SIX PILLARS FROM EPHESIANS

*Experiencing
Jesus*

T.D. JAKES

SIX PILLARS FROM EPHESIANS

Experiencing Jesus

GOD'S SPIRITUAL WORKMANSHIP IN THE BELIEVER

BETHANYHOUSE

MINNEAPOLIS, MINNESOTA

Unless otherwise indicated, all Scripture quotations are taken from the *King James Version* of the Holy Bible.

Scripture quotations marked WUEST are taken from the *New Testament: An Expanded Translation,* by Kenneth S. Wuest. Copyright © 1961 William B. Erdmans Publishing Co., Grand Rapids, Michigan.

Published by Bethany House Publishers
11400 Hampshire Avenue South
Bloomington, Minnesota 55438
www.bethanyhouse.com

Bethany House Publishers is a Division of Baker Book House Company, Grand Rapids, Michigan.

Printed in the United States of America.

Library of Congress Cataloging-in-Publication Data

Jakes, T. D.
  Experiencing Jesus : God's spiritual workmanship in the believer / by T.D. Jakes.
      p.   cm.– (Six pillars from Ephesians ; v. 2) Originally published: Tulsa, Okla. : Albury Pub., c2000. (Jakes, T.D. Six pillars from Ephesians ; v. 2) Originally published: Tulsa, Okla. : Albury Pub., C2000. (Jakes, T.D. Six pillars from Ephesians ; v. 2) Includes bibliographical references.
    ISBN 0-7642-2840-4 (pbk.)
    1. Salvation–Biblical teaching. 2. Bible. N.T. Ephesians–Criticism, interpretation, etc. I. Title II. Series: Jakes, T. D. Six pillars from Ephesians ; v. 2.
    2. Information to come   I. Title
  BS2695.6.S2J34 2003
  227'.506–dc22   2003014734

CONTENTS

EXPERIENCING JESUS
GOD'S SPIRITUAL WORKMANSHIP IN THE BELIEVER

From the moment we are conceived, we have a built-in desire to run the world around us so that it benefits us and serves us completely. Let's face it: We are all born with a self-centered, me-first identity. We emerge from the womb a crybaby, our sole purpose being to see that every whim, desire, and need is fulfilled by those who have obviously been placed in our lives to accomplish this. In our eyes, the world revolves around *us*.

The description I have just given is the essence of the sin nature. There is not one sin we can name that cannot be labeled selfish and self-centered. Furthermore, the original sin is addressed in the first commandment, which contains the antidote to the sin nature:

Thou shalt have no other gods before me.

EXODUS 20:3

God's purpose for our lives is that instead of a me-first identity, we have a God-first identity. We

5

are to step off the throne of our hearts and give God full rule and reign in our lives. We are to throw up our hands in complete surrender to the truth that our well-being, fulfillment, and happiness are totally dependent upon our relationship with Him.

Pride says, "I am the ruler of my own life. I make myself."

Humility says, "God is the ruler of my life. He makes me."

God's Word says:

> **W**e are his workmanship, created in Christ Jesus unto good works.
>
> EPHESIANS 2:10

The issue of God's workmanship in our lives is that it goes against our pride!

In the Psalms, we find a statement that puzzled me for years:

> **E**xcept the Lord build the house, they labor in vain that build it.
>
> PSALM 127:1

I asked myself, "If the Lord is building, why do we have to labor?" The issue was settled when I realized that God is the Master Architect and I am the carpenter. God builds us by design from blueprints drawn up before the foundation of the world. He gives us His plan, and when we labor, our labor must be in alignment with His design or our efforts will fail and have no eternal reward.

Imagine a carpenter looking at the architect's blueprints for a large building project and saying, "Well, that's all good and fine, but I think I'll just add this little wall over here and remove that wall over there and build a wing onto the building over there. Nobody will ever know. I'll just add the plumbing and the wiring and the air-conditioning and heating ducts as I go along. Forget what the architect designed. It's what I want to do."

That carpenter would be removed from the project immediately, and anything he had built according to his own design would be torn down and put in the trash pile. The same principle applies to God's workmanship in our lives. He has the best plan. He sees the end from the beginning and all the battles and obstacles in between. All of our efforts must be in line with His plan for our lives to achieve the maximum joy, purpose, and function.

One of the most important lessons any believer or any body of believers can learn is this: We do not make ourselves. *God makes us.* And when God makes us, He does the full deal! There is no detail too minuscule or crisis too big that He does not provide for our complete redemption from everything that is evil and wicked in this life and the life to come.

Consider Abraham, who had a close encounter of the God kind.

> Now the Lord had said unto Abram, Get thee out of thy country, and from thy kindred, and from thy father's house, unto a land that I will shew thee:
>
> And I will make of thee a great nation, and I will bless thee, and make thy name great; and thou shalt be a blessing:
>
> And I will bless them that bless thee, and curse him that curseth thee: and in thee shall all families of the earth be blessed.
>
> GENESIS 12:1-3

There were seven things God promised Abraham in this passage of Scripture, and one of those was greatness. God said, "I will make your name great." When we first consider that promise, we leap with glee, as most of us desire to be great. However, God's idea of greatness and our idea of greatness may be completely different. For instance, we often think of great men as being wealthy men. But what made Abraham a great man was not necessarily his extensive wealth, although God gave him great wealth. We also think of men who have accomplished supernatural feats as being great. But it might not have been Abraham's ability to sire sons past his productive years, although God gave him that ability, which made him great. Perhaps it wasn't even the fact that he controlled masses of wealth and land, was the guest of noblemen, and was the personal friend to kings in various countries that made Abraham great.

No, if we were to attempt to locate Abraham's greatness, it would probably be more aptly placed in his great faith in God. Called from the Gentile, moon-worshipping country of Ur, Abraham heard God's voice in the wind and had the sensitivity and ability to see the invisible and do the impossible. In any case, whatever the measuring device God uses to determine greatness, the issue for us today is: *Who* made Abraham great?

Why is this such an important question? Because it hits at the heart of the Gospel, which is God's workmanship, not our workmanship, in our lives. We did not call our names out from before the foundation of the world, create ourselves, and when we fell, provide the way of salvation. And neither did we provide the blueprint for our lives. What causes most of us to err and build monuments to our own vanity is that we have a low tolerance for delayed gratification. We do not want to wait on God to make us great. Like Satan, who said his five "I wills" to God in a rebellious declaration of eternal independence (see Isaiah 14:13-14), we say to God,

"You don't have to make me great, I will." For some reason, we really believe we can do it faster and better than God. Oh, the senseless, reasonless, illogical pride of man!

It is that self-imposed, egotistical inclination to exalt oneself that causes us to build walls, churches, companies, and countless other self-designed projects that are not on God's original blueprints or His divine specification sheet. And it is because of this one fact alone that many believers today are experiencing the painful results of being a public success and a private failure. Without faith or patience, they have forsaken God's plan and promise for their lives and turned to their own thinking, when God's plan for them is far beyond their wildest dreams and creativity.

If we have any doubt of the veracity of God's love and faithfulness toward us, our study of Ephesians, chapter 1 — *Loved By God* — will dispel it. Now, in Ephesians 2, the apostle Paul launches into a rich and vivid description of the direct impact Ephesians 1 — all God has accomplished in Christ Jesus — has upon us individually and as a corporate body. We are going to see *how* God makes us, from the moment we are born into His family to the end of time, and on into eternity. And "God don't make no junk!" He always makes us great!

How long has it been since you heard a saint of God glowingly and passionately express their gratitude that God saved them and delivered them from eternal darkness and damnation? If that is all God ever did for us, we have reason to shout and rejoice for the rest of our lives! To comprehend the incredible miracle we have experienced through our new life in Jesus Christ, the apostle Paul begins the second chapter of Ephesians reminding us how despicable and ugly and dark our lives were before the light of Christ made us new and clean and free. We must never forget how our Lord and Savior delivered us from the terrible abyss of spiritual death!

DEATH IS SEPARATION

And you hath he quickened, *who were dead in trespasses and sins;*

11

Wherein in time past ye walked according to the course of this world, according to the prince of the power of the air, the spirit that now worketh in the children of disobedience:

Among whom also we all had our conversation in times past in the lusts of our flesh, fulfilling the desires of the flesh and of the mind; and were by nature the children of wrath, even as others.

EPHESIANS 2:1-3

Dead! We were *dead* in our trespasses and sins. You may notice that the words "hath he quickened" are in italics in your Bible. This is because this phrase was not in the original text. If you read this verse in many other translations, you will find it missing. So verse 1 is simply saying that we were dead in our trespasses and sins. Obviously, because we were still walking around on this earth, "dead" is referring to spiritual death, not physical death.

The Greek word for "dead" is *nekros*, which can mean either the death of the body or the death of the spirit. The word lends itself to the graphic picture of a lifeless, colorless body on a slab in the morgue with the stench of decay surrounding it. You could walk in and poke and prod and scream and yell, but that body is incapable of responding to any stimulus. It is devoid of thought or feeling and has no attachment to the world. It is dead — stinking dead.

Generally in the church today, we have heard and have been taught that before we were born again, we were spiritually dead. But for the Ephesians and for many of us who did not grow up in church, it is startling to hear that before we accepted Jesus as Lord and Savior, we were dead, *nekros* dead. When the Bible talks about death, however, it is not talking about the cessation of life, but separation.

In the case of physical death, the Bible means the separation of the spirit from the body. Death is not the cessation of life in the sense of existence, but the move from one state of being to another. When a person dies and their spirit separates from their body, their spirit will continue to live somewhere, either in heaven or in hell. We thank God that as Christians, to be separated from the body is to be present with the Lord! (See 2 Corinthians 5:8.) When we die and our spirits separate from our bodies, we go to heaven.

To take this a step further, at the point of death, when the spirit separates from the physical body, that body can no longer relate to or function on earth. In like manner, the spirit that is dead is separated from God and cannot relate to or function in the kingdom of God. This state of being spiritually dead is due to our being in trespasses and sins.

Sin separates us from God spiritually and silences our soul.

Are you aware, really aware, that most of the people walking around on the earth today are dead? They may be alive in their flesh, but they are dead in their spirits. They may have a semblance of life in their minds and emotions, but they are under the dominion of death-causing agents: trespasses and sin.

Moreover, Paul tells us that *we were dead* in our trespasses and sins. All of us! We were walking around, thinking, talking, and breathing in trespasses and sins. "Trespasses" is the word *paraptoma*, which we could describe as actions where we slipped off the right path, erred, or wandered away from what is good. "Sins" comes from the Greek word *hamartano*, which literally means "to miss the mark." In ancient Greece, this word was used to describe an athlete who threw a spear and missed the target, the failure of someone to achieve their purpose, or someone simply going wrong.

Paul says, "Remember when we were separated from God? Everything went wrong! No matter what we did or how hard we tried to get it together and make it work and see it through, we continued to miss the mark, to wander from the path, to end up in the wrong place at the wrong time in the wrong crowd. We needed God to guide us out of the darkness and futility of our own way, our own thinking, and even our own desires."

When we were spiritually dead, we may have *acknowledged* God, but we had no intimate *knowledge* of Him. We were dead to Him and separated from Him because of our trespasses and sins. We may have made all sorts of claims to know about God or even may have made claims to understand Him, but no person who is in a state of spiritual death can truly *know* God. Why is this so? Because God cannot have association with sin. He cannot co-exist with something He hates, something which is utterly opposite and opposed to His nature, character, and vision.

It is impossible for a holy and righteous God to coexist with unholy, unrighteous man in the same way it is impossible for light to allow darkness in a room. Remember that God is a giver and a lover, and sin is selfish and self-centered. It seems ironic to the natural mind, but the power of God's love seeks to destroy sin at every turn. God hates the separation sin causes between Himself and mankind. He hates the conflict sin produces between man and man, woman and woman, and man and woman — because He loves us. He loves the sinner and wants the sinner to come to a state of holiness and wholeness in Him.

It was God's love for all of us sinners that provided the remedy for our sin: Jesus, who was without sin, *became* sin on the cross, gave His life and spilt His blood to pay our debt of sin and make a way for us to become right with God. (See Romans 5:17.) But before we accepted this gracious gift of salvation, God could not have intimate fellowship with us, as we were dead and walked in the darkness of our own thoughts and ways.

TWO EVIL FACILITATORS

Paul purposely causes us to look back to the time before we were saved, before we were quickened and made alive by the Holy Spirit. He says, "Do you recognize that we were dead — walking around dead, buying property dead, going to school dead, getting married dead, and having children dead?" We were really not living at all. That's why we were driven to so many different things to try to make us feel alive. We tried to buy life in a bottle or capture it in a drug. We gave all our efforts to a career in hopes that fortune and fame would fill our inner cravings for fulfillment. We tried to find life in a relationship or a series of relationships or just having sex with anyone who would have us.

We tried everything we could think of to make our dead spirit feel alive — and we had plenty of help!

Wherein in time past ye walked according to the course of this world, according to the prince of the power of the air, the spirit that now worketh in the children of disobedience.

EPHESIANS 2:2

Several times in this verse, Paul uses the word *kata*, which is translated "according to." Throughout the Bible, the word *kata* is often translated "with" or "in." It has the connotation of being under the dominion or authority of someone or something. We can walk "according to" the Word of God, under the influence and direction of the Holy Spirit; or we can walk "according to" the world, under the influence and direction of the devil and evil spirits.

In this verse of Scripture, *kata* can also have the connotation of moving downward, of being caught in a downward spiral. Paul is reminding us emphatically that when we were dead in trespasses and sins, everything opposed to God continually worked upon us to pull us down, force us under, make us sink lower and lower, and drive us farther and farther away from God.

When I think of the English word "according," I think of a musical term, "a chord." A chord is a triad of notes that are combined because of their ability to resonate a harmonious sound. Each note is harmonious with the others, and the sound is pleasant to the ear. When we were in harmony with a fallen world, going in the same direction and producing a tone that flowed with the world system, Paul says we walked according to the course of this world. His statement implies that we were in complete harmony with Satan's thinking, nature, and deeds.

Salvation and the very name of Jesus Christ is a dissonant sound to the world system and destroys the continuity of the satanic chord. When we are born again, we begin to sing and love and live in harmony with God's kingdom. The plan for our life becomes His plan and we hook up with His eternal purposes. Therefore, we become a strange, irritating noise to those who are still in concert with the world.

To keep us in harmony with them, the world and satanic forces had one objective from the time we were born: to keep us from receiving Jesus Christ as Lord and Savior. And each second we were dead in trespasses and sins, they drove us to become more and more depraved.

First, we walked according to or were being dominated by the course of this world. In whatever course, whatever lane, or whatever channel the world was going, that's where we were going. You see, just as God's kingdom has ways and rules and principles by which it operates, so does the evil world that opposes Him. A simple example is that while God's kingdom runs on faith, the world system runs on fear. If you read the Bible, you will be filled with faith, but turn on the television or talk to your unsaved neighbors for a while and you will probably be filled with dread and discouragement. The world system floods the earth with negativity, hopelessness, and intimidation.

Another clear distinction is that God's kingdom runs on purity and holiness, but the world system runs on lust and uncleanness (sexual perversion). If you read the Bible, you will be made clean and whole, but go to the movies or a magazine stand in an airport and you will probably be bombarded by filth. The exclusive one-flesh, for-marriage-only, between-a-man-and-a-woman-only sexual relationship according to the Bible is rarely modeled and displayed in the world. According to the world, everybody who's anybody can have sex with anyone they desire because the world encourages an animalistic view of mankind.

Then there is a very subtle and often more evil flip side to this immoral, amoral, and depraved worldly lifestyle. The world system can also keep people away from the saving grace of Jesus Christ by convincing them they are doing "good" and are inherently "good," which is worse!

> **B**ut we are all as an unclean thing, and all our righteousnesses are as filthy rags; and we all do fade as a leaf; and our iniquities, like the wind, have taken us away.
>
> ISAIAH 64:6

When you are in the gutter of sin and depravity you have some idea that you need to be saved! But when you think you're "all that," in church every Sunday, leading the Boy Scouts on Tuesday, and feeding the homeless on Saturday, you are clueless! You have been thoroughly deceived by your good works to believe you are so good, God would never deny you admission to heaven.

It is in this evil flip side that we find the "religious folk." You know who I'm talking about! They look the look and talk the talk and may even seem to walk the walk, but they don't *know* God. Inside they are as dead as the prostitute on the street or the junkie in the alley. The problem is, they don't see it because they are "good folk." Thinking we are good in ourselves is the greatest deception of all, because we do not see our desperate need for God and salvation.

Whether the manifestation of spiritual death is in "good" or evil, the world system is opposed to God's kingdom.

We also walked according to the prince of the power of the air, under the dominion of Satan and his demonic forces. The Greek word translated "prince" is *archon*, which refers to a person or being who is the first one in order of authority, or the leader. Satan's territory is "the air," which most commentators agree is the atmosphere where human beings live. Satan's power is limited, and he operates only as the god of this world, small "g," but we should never underestimate his power!

While we were dead in trespasses and sins, Satan was our spiritual master. His demons were in the air around us, programming us to oppose God, resist Jesus, and walk according to the course of this world. They drove us to waste our lives thinking we were "good," or destroy ourselves and take as many others with us in evil. The Bible tells us that demons operate primarily through our thoughts. That's what I meant when I said that they program us from the time we are born. Many times, what we thought was our own thinking was really demonic. Consider the following "good" and evil thought patterns:

"I can get anything I want" or "I'll never get what I want."

"I'm the best-lookin' thing this world has seen in a long time, and I can have anyone I want" or "I'm so ugly, no one will ever love me."

"I have got what it takes to do anything, and I know I can climb any ladder to success" or "I'm just stupid, and I'll be lucky to get any kind of job."

Here are three examples of the two extremes of satanic thought. For those who Satan knows are prone to be easily discouraged and put down, he repeatedly introduces thoughts of being slighted, ugly, and stupid. For those who he knows are inclined to be very independent and self-assured, he encourages pride and independence from God by telling them they are the best, brightest, and most beautiful.

The devil and his demons enforce the values and principles of the world system in the lives of spiritually dead individuals — and such were we all! If it meant making us happy and successful and feeling good about ourselves to keep us from God, that's how the devil tried to program our thinking. If it meant keeping us in the ghetto, angry, bitter, and blaming everybody but ourselves for our misery, that's what the devil ordered for us. Anything to keep us from Jesus!

CHILDREN OF DISOBEDIENCE

Wherein in time past ye walked according to the course of this world, according to the prince of the power of the air, the spirit that now worketh in the children of disobedience:

Among whom also we all had our conversation in times past in the lusts of our flesh, fulfilling the desires of the flesh and of the mind; and were by nature the children of wrath, even as others.

EPHESIANS 2:2-3

There was a spirit working in us before we were made new by the blood of Jesus Christ, and that spirit epitomized all that the world system and the devil were about. We were children of disobedience, and "disobedience" is the principle word here. It means to be totally uncompliant and unpersuadable. An illustration of this from the Old Testament is when the children of Israel were called "stiff-necked." They turned their backs on God, worshipped idols, did their own thing, and the Word of God fell on deaf ears. They could not be persuaded to listen and were not willing to submit to God's Word.

Writing to the Romans, Paul gives another clear description of "children of disobedience" when he described sinners as being consumed with "uncleanness through the lusts of their own hearts," filled with "vile affections," having a "reprobate mind," and existing in "all unrighteousness." (See Romans 1:24-31.)

Before we were born again, among the children of disobedience in times past, we had our conversation, or lived a lifestyle, by the "lusts of our flesh, fulfilling the desires of the flesh and of the mind." We tried to bring ourselves to life in our flesh! We purchased all kinds of things in hopes that they would make us happy and fulfilled. We drank this, injected that, smoked this, took that pill — just to feel alive. Or we exercised, worked out, took our vitamins, ate healthy, and drank nothing but reverse osmosis water to feel whole and good about ourselves.

In Romans, chapter 1, Paul talks about the final, most terrible state a human being can be in. This is when God eventually gives us over to *ourselves*. One of the worst judgments that can ever be decreed upon us is for us to be left to our own passions and lusts! We become prisoners of our insatiable cravings, striving to fulfill whatever the mind conjures up to satisfy our flesh. That's a bottomless pit called human depravity. Oh, God, if there were no devil and the world was a godly place — *save me from me!* Don't let me be left to merely fulfill the desires of my flesh!

> **F**or as by one man's disobedience many were made sinners, so by the obedience of one shall many be made righteous.
>
> ROMANS 5:19

The Bible tells us that as sons and daughters of Adam, we were born with a nature to sin. Nobody had to teach little Johnny how to lie. Cute little three-year-old, baby-faced, dimple-jawed Johnny climbs up on the counter, steals a cookie, knocks over the cookie jar, and breaks the jar. His mother comes in the kitchen to see that the jar is broken and crumbs are all over Johnny's mouth. She says, "Johnny, did you take a cookie?" And Johnny just shakes his cute little head NOOOOO.

Now, Johnny has not been taking a lying seminar. He has not been listening to lying tapes. There have been no classes in preschool which teach how to lie. Inherently in his nature, under pressure, lying comes out of Johnny because it is down inside of him. He is selfish, self-centered, and self-preserving in the very core of his being because he has a nature to sin!

To be honest, it sounds pretty good to fulfill the desires of our flesh. Hmmmm. It seems to be a really great deal that the mind is responding to the mandates of the flesh, striving to fulfill our every whim and wish. But at the end of all the superficial intimacy, promiscuity, running from place to place, and sinking in the abyss of depravity, there's still that hollowness. We are somewhere down in the basement of our secret lusts and drives and cravings, and after each party's over, there's just that little nagging, aching emptiness — not coming from the flesh or the mind, because the flesh is having a party and the mind is conjuring up new things for next week! The spirit is whispering, "But you're still empty."

"Oh, I got so drunk last night and had such an awesome time!" your flesh declares.

"But you're still empty," whispers your dead spirit.

"What a great workout today. I've never been more together!" your soul cries.

"But you're still empty," whispers your dead spirit.

This is where *all* of us have had our conversations in times past.

CHILDREN OF WRATH

Some of us engaged in all kinds of activities to feel more alive. We clamored for more possessions, more power over others, more experiences, more thrills, and more "highs." Others of us were driven to good works, running all over the place trying to help people and make ourselves feel useful and important. We involved ourselves in all kinds of relationships in hopes that being in love or having a baby or having sex would make us feel more alive. But none of it ever worked in the end. None of it lasted. None of it satisfied. Why? Because none of it ever produced spiritual life!

When all of the self-made efforts were over, there was still something missing in the inner part of our being; there was still a hollow feeling of something being "dead" inside. We were children of wrath. We were warring and seething against all that is holy and pure and selfless by serving the god of self, fulfilling every carnal desire and carrying out every natural inclination — "good" or "evil."

The word "wrath" is translated from the Greek word *orge*, which Aristotle defined as "desire with grief." How fitting for our description of being dead in trespasses and sins! We were cruelly imprisoned by this unholy world system, our jailers being Satan and his evil hoard of demons, and we were subject to the most depraved passions and lusts of our flesh — which only brought us grief.

In these three verses of Scripture, Ephesian 2: 1-3, Paul has painted the darkest and ugliest picture of who we were and how we operated before Christ Jesus entered our lives. I believe the Holy Spirit wants us to grasp with intensity and passion the more-than-imaginable miracle we have experienced in the new birth, when we were liberated from the world system, satanic power, and the eternally dark abyss of our sin nature.

We cannot possibly appreciate the full weight and significance of God's first act of workmanship in our lives — redemption — without understanding what we have been redeemed from. We must never forget the terrible existence, the state of being dead in trespasses and sins, from which God redeemed us through the blood of Jesus Christ!

2

HE QUICKENED US

Consider this phenomenon for a moment: We were dead in our trespasses and sins, controlled by the evil system of this world, under the influence and direction of Satan and demonic forces, driven by our carnal lusts and cravings — and yet we are saved today! How could this be? Satan was supernaturally powerful and much smarter than we were, the world system surrounded us from birth, and we were imprisoned in our carnal, sin nature — yet we somehow managed to escape their deathly grasp. How could this miracle have happened? We were not bright enough, strong enough, or good enough to figure this thing out.

BUT GOD!

But God, who is rich in mercy, for his great love wherewith he loved us,

Even when we were dead in sins, hath quickened us together with Christ, (by grace ye are saved).

EPHESIANS 2:4-5

But God!!!! Thank God for "But God"! Here is a masterful manifestation of God's workmanship in our lives: the new birth, our glorious salvation. We had gone all the way down to the bottom. We had fallen off the bridge with the first man, Adam, had sunk all the way to the gates of hell with condemnation, and the gates of hell opened up their thirsty jaws to engulf us — but God! Paul is talking about the turning point to human depravity. There is no other turning point for human depravity but God.

There is nothing else to fill the emptiness of the human spirit *but God.*

There is no other solution for racial prejudice and injustice *but God.*

There is no other satisfaction for the craving of the flesh and lust *but God.*

There is no healing for the brokenhearted, lonely, and desperate *but God.*

There is no healing for the angry and frustrated *but God.*

There is no way to escape being just like your mother, your father, your grandparents, and subject to all of their curses *but God.*

God's workmanship also brought us to the moment when we would accept Christ Jesus as our Savior and Lord. He didn't allow us to be aborted or miscarried! He didn't allow us to be stillborn, to die of crib death, or to be killed by any number of childhood accidents or diseases. He never took His hand off our lives. It doesn't matter if we were abused or rejected as a child. God brought us through that experience alive and kept us from losing our sanity. He brought us to an understanding of Jesus Christ as our Savior and raised us up so that we could *still* fulfill His purpose and reflect His glory in spite of every effort of the devil to destroy us, diminish us, defame us, or discourage us.

The "But God" element in Ephesians is the breaking of the first and original generational curse. It is proof positive that God can break the downward spiral of a family of sin. Adam's sin caused the greatest and perhaps the only generational curse that matters. Had he produced a son before he fell into sin, he would have started the "chosen generation" that Jesus Christ ultimately established. But alas, it was in his fallen, degenerate state that his first two sons, Cain and Abel, were born. When Cain slew Abel, we see the fruit of the already-operating, downward spiral of sin, and you and I are just another member of the fallen family. We were born like all of Adam's sons — with contaminated blood! Our blood was contaminated with the sin nature.

We were born dead, stillborns in the womb of life, but God quickened us. The quickening Spirit of God fell upon us like a paramedic rushes to the scene of a crime, finding a world asphyxiated by its overindulgence and lacking the breath of God. The word "spirit," translated from *pneuma* in the Greek, is often translated "air." There we were, "code-blue" stillborns, our pale and lifeless bodies dead on His table, and the Holy Spirit breathed the divine air of God Almighty into us. From that moment, quickened and made alive forever, all the curses from our natural father, Adam, were broken. When Jesus went to His cross, He forever altered what had been the tragic saga of a fallen family.

The "But God" in Ephesians turns a tragedy into a fairy tale. It is the sudden happy ending that seemed so far away from us before we knew Jesus. Without "But God," hell would have had a party! "But God" was the turning point in our story. It started with Him, who is rich in mercy, and the Greek word for "rich" means to literally be fabulously wealthy, to be overwhelmed with goods. God had an unlimited, overabundance of mercy and chose to lavish it on us. With the new birth, He broke the bank for us!

For ye know the grace of our Lord Jesus Christ,
that, though he was rich, yet for your sakes he became
poor, that ye through his poverty might be rich.

2 CORINTHIANS 8:9

ALIVE TO GOD

There was that magnificent moment in time
when everything came together and we recognized
two truths simultaneously: we could not possibly
fill the eternal cavern of emptiness within ourselves,
but God just might be able to. At that point, which
was for many of us a time of deepest despair or
futility, we turned to receive the richness of His
mercy and the greatness of His love. We surrendered our lives to Jesus Christ and God "hath
quickened us together with Christ." Literally, God
made our dead spirit alive with the same power
with which He resurrected Jesus from the dead!
Revelation 1:5 declares that Jesus was the *firstborn
from the dead,* the first to be "quickened."

The word "quickened" means "to be made alive."
When we were born again, the Spirit of God took
up residence in us and quickened or breathed His
eternal life into our dead spirit. Without God's
Spirit, my spirit was dead, but when the Holy
Spirit moved into my spirit, He quickened my
spirit and I became alive in the innermost parts of

33

my being! My spirit became alive with the life of God! His Spirit and my spirit are now living in relationship together, in covenant together. In Him I live and move and have my being, awareness, and consciousness. I am awake to the glory of God in my spirit. That all by itself is shouting material!

The Spirit of God came into your heart, quickened you, and like a sleeping giant emerging out of a cave, you woke up and became aware of a God who was there all the time. When Jacob discovered God, he said, *"Jehovah Shamma, God is present and I knew it not."* (See Genesis 28:16.) Remember if you can, or consider right now, that moment when you first *felt* the presence of God in your life, when the Spirit of God bore witness with your spirit that you were His child and your heart cried, "Abba, Father!" Is there anything more exciting and fulfilling in life than being alive to God? If that was all there was to the new birth it would be worth it! But God doesn't stop there.

At the moment we are quickened by the Holy Spirit and made alive to God, we receive all the wealth and spiritual blessings Paul describes to us in Ephesians, chapter 1. Now being alive to God, His Word comes alive and leaps off the pages into our hearts, and the Holy Spirit begins to whisper all the glorious realities of our new life in Christ. We are alive to the fullness of God:

- He chose us from before the foundation of the world to be holy and blameless before Him in love.

- He predestined us to be His precious adopted children because it was His greatest pleasure to do so.

- In His tremendous grace toward us, He made us accepted in the Beloved, no longer desperate for love or devastated at the rejection of men, but fulfilled and contented in Him.

- He gloriously redeemed us from being dead in our trespasses and sins, forgave every transgression, and chose to forget them forever.

- He lavished upon us the abundance of all His wisdom and prudence so we could operate effectively and skillfully in life.

- Again, because it was His pleasure to do so, He revealed to us the mystery of His will: the gathering together of all things in heaven and earth as one in Christ Jesus.

- He declared that we are His inheritance, and He has our lives worked out so that we will bring Him nothing but praise and glory because we trust in Him.

- He sealed us with the Holy Spirit, setting His mark upon us for all to see that we belong to Him and Him alone.

Is your heart not jumping out of your chest at the revelation of all you have been given as a child of God?

You see, we were quickened "together with Christ." In God's eyes, which see from eternity past through eternity future, all those who are in Christ — past, present, future — are the body of Christ resurrected. When God resurrected Jesus from the grave, He resurrected all of us with Him. Therefore, when we were quickened, all the wealth and spiritual blessings of Christ became ours. Hallelujah!

Now, wouldn't it be terrible for you to work like a dog to give everything you have to your children, and they did not use what you gave them? It must be frustrating to be God, to go through so much to empower us and enrich us, and then to watch us murmuring and complaining as if we didn't have what He died to give us. It must be terrible to be God and have to sit up every night and hear us praying for Him to do what He has already done, to see us wallow in problems that He's already given us power to overcome. We stand there as if our hands are tied, saying, "God, You've got to do something," when He did it all 2,000 years ago!

This is the great love wherewith He has loved us. He didn't wait for us to cry for help. In eternity past He anticipated our need and delivered us.

Federal Express brought a package to my house the other day and I wasn't home, so they left a note on the door that said, "We could not deliver." That doesn't mean they didn't have the package or that the person didn't send the package. It simply means that deliverance was not complete because I did not receive the package. Deliverance is when our wealthy God delivers a package to us and we receive what He has given. When we reach out and take hold of what God has done for us in the new birth, we surrender to His workmanship in our lives and our deliverance is complete.

Many times when people become Christians, one of the hardest things to do is to retrain them not to continue to operate according to the world system, the prince of the power of the air, and their old sin nature now that they're quickened in their spirit and alive to God. Like Israel, God delivered them out of Egypt, but it took years to get Egypt out of them. Often we come out of our conversation in times past (see Ephesians 2:3) and find a new battle is taking place, between the old man and the new man. Thank God, this is a battle He has given us the equipment and strength and wisdom to win!

That's why we need teaching like this in Ephesians. We must continually be challenged, slapped in the face, and awakened by God's Word and His Spirit that we are not dead anymore! God's very life has entered our inner man and quickened us. We don't have to operate in bondage to sin anymore. We don't have to respond to anger in a self-destructive manner anymore. It's no longer necessary for us to get others "straightened out" and going our way. No more do we have to flip out on people and operate in our flesh. We can be free of our mother's temper and our father's rage and all of the things that operated in us because our spirit was dead. Because God has breathed into us the breath of life, we are no longer controlled by generational curses, the systems of this world, or our depraved flesh. We have to *know and continually be aware* that we are miraculously and supernaturally changed by God on the inside!

UNDER NEW MANAGEMENT

One of the most amazing things to me is when I hear Christians lobbying and fighting and arguing, trying to get Christian principles in the world system. It just blows my mind that we somehow think we can get sinners to live like saints. We're having a great enough challenge getting the saints to live like saints! How have we managed to confuse morality with regeneration?

Regeneration will produce morality, but any attempt at morality without regeneration only produces hypocrisy and arrogance, which are still the fruit of a dead spirit. We Christians often confuse the work of the Holy Spirit in us, thinking it is something we did. The reality is that without God, we can do nothing! If someone is not quickened by the Holy Spirit in their spirit and alive to God, they are caught in the wind of the world system, tossed to and fro by a myriad of demonic lies, and lost in the sea of their lusts and prejudices. They really can't help it. The carnal mind is enmity, or at war, against God. It is out of harmony with Him, unquickened, and unregenerated, and cannot receive the things of God.

So what happens when the brothers and sisters come pointing their fingers at them, yelling at them, and telling them to live a different way? They don't even understand what the saints are talking about! Rhetoric and debate cannot correct a heart problem. We cannot pass a bill that makes people love one another. Only when the Church steps out of the political arena, goes back into the pulpit, and hits the streets to preach the glorious

Gospel of Jesus Christ will the hearts of men be changed and our world transformed.

If we could fix men from the outside in, then Buddha or Confucius or Aristotle would have been effective. All of the great thinkers of the ages would have been able to approach people through thinking and mind power, challenging them with principles and concepts to change their behavior. But our message is, "Verily, verily I say unto you, ye must be born again, recreated in your spirit by Christ Jesus."

We must live in the reality that we have moved to a different kingdom and are under different management. We have changed residences and have been given a brand-new identity on the inside of us. Then we must allow God to work within us and work out from within us our salvation, and that takes some "fear and trembling"! Under the new management of God, we are continuously standing on the edge of eternity until Jesus returns. Our perspective has gone beyond just the here and now to how the here and now fits into God's plan for all the ages.

Now we have a new and easier yoke and burden, which allow us to come to grips with and begin to live in and enjoy all the wealth of Ephesians, chapter 1. This is another aspect of God's work-manship in us: to become like Jesus. When we become like Jesus, the world will take notice! They will come to our door and ask us to pray for them. They will want to be around us because they sense in their dead spirit that our spirit is alive to God. The greatest impact we can have on the world is to fully submit to God's workmanship in our lives.

UNIQUENESS WITHIN

When you received Jesus as your personal Lord and Savior, God breathed His Spirit into you, making you a new creature. God is your Creator, and you are a designer original! God made you a one-of-a-kind creation who is so unique and precious, you are priceless. He made you brand-new on the inside, and the greatest adventure for eternity is discovering who you are in Him.

The uniqueness of your spirit is mirrored in the uniqueness of your physical attributes. You have a fingerprint that is unlike that of anybody else. The same goes for your footprint, handprint, voiceprint, and your entire genetic code. Nobody else has ever had the combination of physical traits you have. Nobody else has your precise set of genes.

Nobody else has been placed by God in your family, your neighborhood, with your friends, in your church, and in your city. Nobody else like you has been put on the earth with exactly the same set of talents, personality quirks, strengths, weaknesses, abilities, and disabilities that you have. He knows the length of your days and the outer limits of your potential.

God designed you with facets and dimensions that you may not even know! When the Holy Spirit came to abide in you, He made you alive to God and gave you spiritual gifts and spiritual fruit. Now you can desire the best gifts and operate in them as the Spirit wills. You can draw on the fruit of the Holy Spirit inside you: love, joy, peace, longsuffering, gentleness, goodness, faith, meekness, and temperance. And what is all this for? Now that you are alive to God, you are obligated to bring that life to others. (See 2 Corinthians 1:3-4.) This is called the ministry of reconciliation.

You have been made a minister of reconciliation, as we are all ministers of reconciliation. (See 2 Corinthians 5:18.) You may never stand in the pulpit of a church, but you are called to preach and teach the Gospel, to heal the sick, to cast out demons, and to make disciples in whatever walk of life God has called you. All of this was deposited into you at the moment of the new birth!

So many people I meet are not happy with the workmanship of God in their lives because they are forever comparing themselves to others, wanting to be like others. It is a slap in God's face to look at another person and say, "I want to be like them." God tenderly and uniquely designed you to be just the way He wanted you to be. He made you for Himself and He made you in a way that can never be duplicated.

When you compare yourself to another person, you are saying to God, "You made a mistake. You failed in making me. You could have done a better job." No one has the privilege or right to criticize God in that way. He is the Creator who looks at each of His created beings and says to Himself, "It is good." You being *you* gives Him the utmost pleasure!

Why is it so important that we understand our uniqueness in Christ? Because we are a *body*, the body of Christ, and God's desire is to empower us to reach a lost and dying world *together*. He wants to *quicken* the Church! But He cannot empower and quicken a body where the foot wants to be the hand and the eyes want to be the ears and the elbow wants to be the knee. We must rest in His workmanship in us as individuals so that He can move us forward corporately. Then we can be His glorious Church, showing forth to the world how they too can be quickened and made alive to God.

God's workmanship was evident when we were dead in trespasses and sins in that He brought us to salvation despite the pressures and influences of the world, the devil, and our flesh. His workmanship is then revealed in a majestic and awesome fashion, as He is the Creator of our born-again spirit, quickening us and making us alive to Him. Now that we are quickened and under His management, He is bringing us and will continue to bring us through a specific set of situations and circumstances to complete His purpose, reflect His glory — and just to give Him delight. For this, He built into us the capacity to grow and develop and change and adapt. He gave us the potential to become like Jesus.

God's present workmanship in our lives is conforming us to the image of Christ Jesus. Now, we don't have to get all freaked out and feel like we are losing our uniqueness and identity as individuals, because that is not what being conformed to the image of Jesus means!

> *For whom he did foreknow, he also did predestinate to be conformed to the image of his Son, that he might be the firstborn among many brethren.*

ROMANS 8:29

The word "conformed" is translated from the Greek word *summorphos*. This word means more than just to be fashioned in the likeness or image of someone. It actually goes beyond the superficial outward appearance and denotes an inward conformity. In practical terms, what this is saying is that we are not being made into an exact clone or replica of Jesus, but we are to express ourselves from the innermost parts of our being as He does. We are to love as He loves, be moved with compassion as He is moved with compassion, abide in God's Word as He abides in God's Word, and follow the leading of the Holy Spirit as He follows the leading of the Holy Spirit.

The concept of being conformed to the image of Jesus Christ is made real to us in Ephesians 2:4-7. After God moves on us in our dead state and quickens us, He then places us in a spiritual position for all eternity that enables us to be conformed to the image of Jesus while we are in this earth.

WHO ARE "US"?

But God, who is rich in mercy, for his great love wherewith he loved us,

Even when we were dead in sins, hath quickened us together with Christ, (by grace ye are saved;)

And hath raised us up together, and made us sit together in heavenly places in Christ Jesus:

That in the ages to come he might shew the exceeding riches of his grace in his kindness toward us through Christ Jesus.

EPHESIANS 2:4-7

One of the benefits of our position in Christ is that we are being conformed into His image! Literally, our outlook on life, our demeanor, and the manner in which we react to situations are starting to look like and act like what Jesus would do in the same situations. Even more importantly, God is dealing with us to emulate the relationship He has with His Son, Jesus Christ. God wants us to come into oneness, not just with Him, but with each other. Our position demands that we become like God. While that is impossible for us to accomplish on our own, our position in Christ brings with it the power and ability to be who we are in Him.

As we consider the term "us" in these verses of Scripture, the question arises, "Who are the 'us' of the text?" It causes us to reflect on the phrase "quickened us together," in the fifth verse. If He has quickened us together, we must know who we are quickened together with. We are no longer considering the individual being made alive through faith in Jesus Christ. Now Paul is talking about us being quickened together. "Together" reassures us that we are speaking of a joining of more than one in this quickening.

If we miss this important truth, we will walk away from the second chapter completely ignorant of Paul's heart for reconciliation in the body of Christ. He is building a case that will show that the Church is the only entity on earth and in heaven that not only tears down the wall of partition between Jew and Gentile, but also quickens the two together in Christ. Do you see that there is a dynamic, supernatural union being described here?

Paul's heart is to show that the Church is not Jew or Gentile, but the joining together of the two as one body in Christ Jesus. This is a theme he later illustrates by describing the mystery of the marriage union. Just as the man and the woman become one in holy matrimony, the once idolatrous Gentiles are joined with the chosen people of the old covenant. As children with hearts open only to their Savior and hands clasped with one another and raised in praise to their God, they are quickened together by grace into this marvelous new dimension we call the Church. The "us" are one in Christ.

God gives a graphic picture of His grace exhibited in opulent style as it is painted on the canvas of the Gentile heart. Gentiles whose immorality and perversion polluted the streets with debauchery and degradation are permitted to be joined with a people who have walked devoutly with Jehovah in the Old Testament. Gentiles who were separated from the commonwealth of Israel and the covenant of God are now not only connected to it, but are quickened into a new institution of grace, the Church.

We will see as the chapter progresses that Paul will close it with the theme of people being joined together, for it is this divine union which forms a

habitation of God through the spirit. The God who
quickens "us" together in the early parts of chapter 2
now dwells in that corporate gathering by verse 22.
The twain become one. They become an "us."
Without developing the "us" mentality, the Church
will be forever divided by races, denominations, and
creeds — unable to be that holy habitation of God.

It was Paul's intent both in Ephesians as well as in
Romans to explain that this is where the enemy
builds the strongest breach in the body of Christ. It
is an attempt to divide us so that God's presence
and power can never manifest in our individual and
corporate lives. This breach is between brothers. It
is not Cain against Adam. It is Cain against Abel. It
is not Jacob against Isaac. It is Jacob against Esau.
Our struggle is not just reconciliation with God,
but reconciling with our brothers and sisters. This
principle is so vital, Jesus told us:

> Therefore if thou bring thy gift to the altar, and there
> rememberest that thy brother hath ought against thee;
> Leave there thy gift before the altar, and go thy
> way; first be reconciled to thy brother, and then come
> and offer thy gift.

MATTHEW 5:23-24

Do not try to be quickened with God when you
will not be reconciled with your brother! While I
realize Paul's focus in Ephesians 2 is on Gentiles and

Jews, I also realize that God's workmanship in the Church will always require that twain become one. When we come to grips with the fact that God is not interested in selfish individual agendas, but moves in a corporate vision, then and only then will we know the mystery and dynamism of the "us."

In essence, God is calling us to love one another as He has loved us.

POSITION IS EVERYTHING

There is an element of God's workmanship which is one of the biggest challenges and deepest mysteries in the Christian life, and that is understanding His awesome love for us. His love for us has the biggest impact on us as individuals and on the body of Christ as a whole than any other aspect of our relationship with Him. Ephesians 2:4-7 gives us a dramatic illustration of His love, that even when we were dead in our trespasses and sins, God quickened us. He loved us when we were dead! Remember the dead body on the slab in the morgue? That was us — stinking, decayed, and lifeless. But He loved us dead and breathed His life into us. He brought us out of death and darkness into eternal life and light.

God's love for us goes far beyond human understanding, and that is why Paul says it twice in one

verse: "for his great love wherewith he loved us."
When you read something twice in a row in the
Bible, you can be certain the Holy Spirit is empha-
sizing something that is extremely important.
Whenever Jesus says, "Verily, verily," that means,
"Listen up now and listen up good!"

Then the apostle Paul makes the statement every
believer knows so well: "for by grace ye are saved."
The word "saved" is the Greek word *sesosmenoi*,
which literally translated would be "in a saved state"
or "being saved." The Greek construction here
indicates that God saved us completely at a point in
time in our past, yet our salvation continues in the
present. The way Paul has worded this is both
dramatic and emphatic. He is telling us that every
breath of our salvation breathed in our present is
due only to the grace by which we were saved in
the past. In this way, no matter what takes place,
there is no one to receive the glory but Jesus.

The workmanship of God in our lives through
grace is inestimable. We will discuss the grace of
God in more depth in the next chapter, but for now
I must interject this. The apostle Paul is the "grace
man" of the New Testament, and his epistles are
laced with grace throughout. Anywhere and every-
where he could mention the fact that we are saved

by grace and kept by grace, he does so, and this is one of those places!

Now, in verse 6, Paul describes our new position as a child of God. In one motion He raises us, and in the next motion He makes us sit. Those are two different things. First, to be raised up from that lower state of being dead in trespasses and sins is to be placed over the world system, the prince of the power of the air, and our old sin nature. We have come to a place of authority and power over the very things that once held us captive and kept us in bondage. That is good news!

Then, we are seated with Jesus in the heavenlies. Now, whenever we are sitting, it means we're not moving, because we cannot move as long as we sit. God raised us up and never said anything about going down again! It was not His intention that we go down and then be raised up and go down and then be raised up again. He raised us up and then made us sit, period. That's because He has placed us in a position to be stable. Remember, the wolf is coming! But when the wolf comes, he will find us *sitting* in heavenly places — not shaken, not moved, and not disturbed, but stable.

Sitting is a position, not a transition. If we are in transition, we are not sitting! When we sit, that means we are here for as long as God wants us here.

We have entered into a position in God that we refuse to forfeit for anybody or anything because we have arrived at the place where we are going to abide and stay and not be moved.

This is our position in Christ right now and in every circumstance of life. I often say that most Christians today are preoccupied with their condition when they should be consumed by their position. They rejoice when they get a check in the mail and shout, "Ooooh, He blessed me today!" They get up and testify, "The lump is gone! I can't find the lump!" Those are conditions. They are temporal things. And I have news for any person who gets healed: You're going to have to fight for your health again! You may have received a check today, but you're going to need some more money tomorrow.

When we celebrate our condition, we are majoring in the minor and ignoring the major, our position. When we start focusing on our position, we will be standing on a foundation the devil can't shake. Our conditions change from moment to moment, and it is wonderful and grand when we pray and the Holy Spirit comes in and changes and rearranges things for our good. But the reason we can pray for conditions to change is because of our position, and our position is eternal! We need to be praising and worshipping God that we have been raised up and are sitting with Him in the heavenlies!

When we praise God for our condition, we call attention to today. We get happy about God and what He is doing for us right now. But when we praise God for our position, we call attention to eternity, and we move into a whole new dimension of praise and worship!

GOD LOVES TO SHOW OFF

After the apostle Paul describes our new position, he tells us the reason for it:

> *That in the ages to come he might shew the exceeding riches of his grace in his kindness toward us through Christ Jesus.*

EPHESIANS 2:7

God wants to show off! Do you know that God delights in doing the impossible and He is the best showman who ever existed? P. T. Barnum had nothing on God. Houdini and all these high-tech magicians today can't touch the riches of God's grace expressed toward mankind through the ages. Who can top the parting of the Red Sea and the resurrection of Jesus Christ? When God makes a point, He makes it with style!

But this verse is not just talking about the "big" things God has done. This is about you and me! He wants to show *us* off in the ages to come. Now we must get on our eternal caps and start thinking in eternal terms. That's kind of hard to do because eternity is hard to imagine, and our minds are bound by time and space. We can't even remember all of our time as it is. You know you don't remember what you did when you were three months old, and I don't remember what I did yesterday! So when we start talking about eternity, it's difficult for the human mind to fathom, but Paul says there are going to be ages to come. We need to quit stressing out about this little moment we're in and realize there is much, much more to come.

> **F**or our light affliction, which is but for a moment, worketh for us a far more exceeding and eternal weight of glory;
> While we look not at the things which are seen, but at the things which are not seen: for the things which are seen are temporal; but the things which are not seen are eternal.

2 CORINTHIANS 4:17-18

Paul says that what we are going through now has significance and meaning because we weigh it in light of eternity and not in terms of our present condition and comfort. If we look at our lives through the eyes of God and focus on the eternal

55

things which are not seen by the natural eye, God will work in us a far greater glory in eternity. In the ages to come He will show the riches of His grace by saying, "Look at how I saved them. Look at all they did wrong, how they sinned and were stinking and dead, and I saved them." God is going to prove His goodness through our badness!

Now I'm really going to get down into a little groove here, and I hope you can take this! God even means for people to talk about your past! I know you don't want anybody to do that, but it's necessary. You see, God had enough sense to know that when He saved you, somebody would know something about you. And He's going to use what was against you for His glory. Take the lame man who was at the gate called Beautiful in Acts 3:2-10, for example. He sat there all the time, and everybody thought that was as far as he was going to go. Then one day Peter and John came through at the hour of prayer and Peter said, "Silver and gold have I none; but such as I have give I thee: In the name of Jesus Christ of Nazareth rise up and walk!" (v. 6).

We all know what happened. That lame man jumped up on his weak, lifeless feet and came walking and leaping and praising God right through the temple. But the first thing everyone said was, "Is this the man who sat outside the gate?

Isn't he the same beggar we passed by all these years?" God used that man's past for His glory.

Jesus told one lame man to take up his bed and walk. *Well,* I thought to myself, *if He was going to heal him, why didn't He just let him leave his bed?* If I had been lying in the bed and had been carried in by four men, I'd want to leave the bed and go to running! But Jesus said, "Take up your bed and walk," because He wanted to use that bed in the man's arms to say that the thing that had carried him, he was now carrying. Are you seeing what I'm saying here? He will use our scars to become His stars!

This concept of God using your past for His glory is for people who have matured enough to see the master plan. Jonah's disobedience and his incarceration in the belly of a whale was what Jesus used to be a picture of His death, burial, and resurrection. Jonah was in the belly of the fish for three days as Jesus was in the belly of the earth for three days. Jonah didn't know that one of the reasons he was there was so Jesus could use his failure to preach His message.

"That in the ages to come, He might show the exceeding riches of His glory." God will say throughout eternity, "Look how much I did with so little." If we look back over our lives and examine our successes and all the things we have acquired, we know it is the grace of God in our lives. People think we're smart, but we know we weren't that smart. They think we're just so talented and so gifted, but we know that all the creativity and drive they see is being drawn from the very heart of God.

God did so much with so little! After a while He's just going to put us in His curio chest and show us off and say, "Look what I did! Look at My workmanship. Can you believe that I made this glorious creature out of clay? Can you believe that is something I scooped up out of the ground, and it wouldn't even hold water when I first picked it up, but I kept on molding it and raising it up until it achieved its destiny."

They tell me that when a potter begins working with clay on a potter's wheel, he never presses down; he always raises the lump of clay up. His hands are continually touching the clay as it spins around, and he is fashioning it into the masterpiece he desires, giving it the form and features which will fulfill its purpose.

For eternity, God will point to us and declare, "Look what I raised up out of nothing! Although their whole life was spinning, I never let go of them, and I raised them up and sat them in the heavenlies. And now these vessels are holding water! They are holding relationships and ministries

and concepts and a job and their integrity and
getting their life together. They couldn't have done
that without My workmanship in their lives. What
you heard about them was true, they were a disgrace
and a disaster, but My grace was sufficient. And
now they are sitting here with Me forever."

> And we know that all things work together for good
> to them that love God, to them who are the called
> according to his purpose.
> For whom he did foreknow, he also did predestinate
> to be conformed to the image of his Son, that he might
> be the firstborn among many brethren.
>
> ROMANS 8:28-29

We were raised and seated by the Great Potter
of the Universe to be conformed in our inner man
to the image of Christ Jesus, and it is our position in
Christ which is the source of everything we are and
everything we do in the Christian life. From this
powerful spiritual position, our spirit man continually breathes the life of God and receives all the
spiritual blessings for the moment, for the day, for
the time in which we live, and forever.

Whenever we feel the world and the devil trying
to pull us down into that former spiral of death and
darkness, we must only remember where we sit!

4
HE GRACED US

When Saul of Tarsus was saved on the road to Damascus, God sent a man named Ananias to pray for him. But because Saul was a well-known persecutor of the Church, Ananias was horrified to even go near Saul. So the Lord comforted Ananias with these words:

> **B**ut the Lord said unto him, Go thy way: for he is a chosen vessel unto me, to bear my name before the Gentiles, and kings, and the children of Israel:
>
> For I will shew him how great things he must suffer for my name's sake.

ACTS 9:15-16

STEWARD OF GRACE

From the moment he was saved, Paul knew that he would suffer great things for the Gospel's sake and that God had called him to preach to the Gentile first, then to kings, and finally to the Jew.

Before he was separated by the Holy Spirit for this full-time ministry, however, he spent many years studying the Word of God and being taught of the Holy Spirit. Furthermore, there was one particular revelation Paul received which was essential to his ministry and would truly become the hallmark of his teaching. This was the revelation of the grace of God.

> **F**or this cause I Paul, the prisoner of Jesus Christ for you Gentiles,
> If ye have heard of the dispensation of the grace of God which is given me to you-ward:.....
> Unto me, who am less than the least of all saints, is this grace given, that I should preach among the Gentiles the unsearchable riches of Christ.
>
> EPHESIANS 3:1-2, 8

So passionate was Paul concerning the issue of grace, he nearly came to blows over the matter on several occasions with Peter and the legalistic Jews. In fact, many scholars believe that Paul's thorn in the flesh was actually a faction of religious Jews who had received Jesus as Messiah, referred to as Judaizers. They followed Paul wherever he went, endeavoring to turn his Gentile converts from the simple Gospel of being saved by grace to a gospel of being saved by works of the Jewish laws and traditions.

Paul would go into a city, preach the Gospel, and see many Gentiles saved by grace and set free.

Then these Judaizers would come in after him and tell the people they weren't really saved unless they observed all the Jewish laws. What Paul had established in the liberty of grace would become a dead, ritualistic work. This totally exasperated the apostle, and he wrote the book of Galatians specifically to eradicate all claims of the law on the Gospel. Galatians is essentially a theological treatise on the importance of grace in both salvation and our Christian walk. He clearly outlines the doctrine of grace once and for all.

Paul takes full responsibility for delivering the dispensation of the grace of God to the Church. He is a master builder who is continuously conferring with the Architect to make certain that he is giving the accurate blueprint and specs to the carpenters in his employ. His obligation and joy are to make sure that the Church is built according to God's plan of grace. A good scripture to illustrate this is:

> **S**tudy to shew thyself approved unto God, a workman that needeth not to be ashamed, rightly dividing the word of truth.
>
> 2 TIMOTHY 2:15

The analogy Paul uses here is of a journeyman carpenter who takes a piece of wood that has just been cut by his apprentice and looks down the line to make sure that the cut is straight. Anybody who has ever done any building knows there is a constant conferring back and forth between the architect, the builder, the carpenters, and journeymen to make sure the master blueprint is being meticulously and faithfully followed. So when Paul talks about being a steward here, he doesn't just pen the words or draw up the specs and walk away and leave the carpenter on his own. Nor does he cease conferring with the Architect. He continues to communicate with both and have proprietorship over what is being developed to maintain continuity.

When Paul says, "For this cause I am a prisoner," he means, "I can't just walk away from this thing. I am committed to this dispensation of grace and will make sure that it is completely developed and maintains its purity and power." To do that, Paul also made certain that he was imparting this revelation into the hearts of faithful men. These were men who were committed, not fly-by-night people who just wanted to impress people with rhetoric. These were the devout and faithful who had a passion for the truth and the same godly drive Paul had to see the Church built according to God's plan.

MORE THAN UNMERITED FAVOR

For Paul, the grace of God was the most essential component of God's salvation program. Preaching, teaching, and defending the unadulterated, untampered grace of God was the very mission of his ministry. But what is grace? Those of us who have grown up in church could easily pull out our standard definition of grace: "God's unmerited favor." This cryptic three-word definition is a feeble attempt to explain this grand and glorious aspect of salvation.

Paul was so dedicated to the concept of grace that he used the term three times as much as all of the rest of New Testament literature! The word "grace" comes from the Greek word *charis*. Its original definition was "pure joy or pleasure." The idea was that something was done to another person that was pleasurable but undeserved. Out of the utmost and greatest joy, God blesses us for no other reason than it gives Him pleasure.

Grace, then, is the term that represents the attitude and manner in which God provides our salvation. The flow is as follows: God forms man out of the dust of the ground and breathes into man the breath of life. This breathing and forming aspect of God's creation is significant in that all the other components of God's creation came into existence by His spoken Word. But man is brought into being by intimate and personal contact with God. He invests in His human creation His image and likeness and very Spirit. This is supposed to be a relationship of great fellowship, sharing, and caring. God will display His glory and magnificence, and man, having the ability to observe, experience, and process that kind of information, will worship Him for it.

Instead, man blatantly sins against the commandments of God. He dies spiritually and is separated from God, is expelled from the Garden of Eden, and begins to suffer the consequences of his actions. While God has all the evidence of the depravity of man to justifiably destroy him, He instead works out an elaborate program of salvation.

The apostle Paul is fascinated by the contrasts found in this history. Humanity is totally incapable of rehabilitating themselves. They cannot produce anything of sufficient value to reverse the sentence of death assigned to them, and they find themselves totally at the mercy of God. At the same time, God is angry with the wicked, and His holy nature will not allow Him to simply overlook their violations and declare man saved. He hates and must destroy sin, but He loves man. The mighty God resolves this problem by offering His Son, Jesus Christ, as a sinless sacrifice to be a substitute for all of mankind. His Son's death satisfies His wrath against sinning mankind, divine justice is served, and through Jesus Christ man has a way back to God and godliness. This is the synopsis of the Gospel message.

As exciting as the substitutionary sacrifice of Jesus Christ is, Paul cannot rest until he has revealed another great facet of this wonderful salvation — grace. Man's totally depraved nature and absolute need for a savior is met with the substitutionary work of Jesus Christ on the cross and in the resurrection. The "pure joy and pleasure," grace, or *charis* of God Himself brought forth deliverance to the human race. His delight to save and make whole again brought forth the atonement through His Son.

> **L**ooking unto Jesus the author and finisher of our faith, who for the joy that was set before him endured the cross, despising the shame, and is set down at the right hand of the throne of God.
>
> HEBREWS 12:2

It was for joy (again the Greek word is *charis*) that Jesus endured the cross, and that joy set before Him was you and me! This is the grace with which God brings forth our salvation. The doctrine of grace becomes the backdrop and the framework of our salvation and describes the mindset of God when He brought about our redemption. God's grace is at the very heart of His workmanship in us.

GRACE REVEALED

One of the best Bible stories to use to describe grace is the story of the adulterous woman in John, chapter 8, one of my favorite passages. This unnamed woman is forceably brought to Jesus. She has been caught in the "very act" of adultery. Her prosecutors ask for only one thing from Jesus — His permission to execute her.

What do you think is going on in her mind? She is standing there in front of a man who is going to decide whether she lives or dies. She has no lawyer, no legal war chest, and not even a character witness to take her side. She is guilty and she knows it. Her prosecutors know it, and it is generally known in her community. The evidence is clear and convincing.

This adulteress has nothing to offer in exchange for her freedom, nothing to say that will persuade the man to exonerate her, and no hope of escaping a terrible death by stoning. She is done for. The prosecutors are hard-nosed and unyielding, the law is clear and precise concerning such a crime, and the man she is facing is known to be meticulously fair and honest. He, it would seem, has no alternative but to agree to her execution.

While she waits for her ears to report what the rest of her being already knows will be the verdict, her eyes show her a strange sight. Her judge stoops to the ground and begins to scribble something on the ground. When He finishes this exercise, all of her accusers disappear. The indictment against her lies on the prosecution table unattended. The judge invites her to join in the search for her accusers, and when she cannot locate them, He says to her, "Neither do I accuse you. Go and sin no more."

That's the grace of God revealed to us! Jesus took her from a position of undeniable guilt and an irrevocable sentence to a totally free and unconditional pardon. That's grace! She did nothing to deserve this kindness; she had nothing with which to purchase this kindness, and she didn't even know that such a thing was possible. That's grace!

> **F**or by grace are ye saved through faith; and that not of yourselves: it is the gift of God:
> Not of works, lest any man should boast.
>
> EPHESIANS 2:8-9

Paul celebrated this grace, cherished this grace, and dedicated his entire ministry to the cause of presenting the grace message to believers. He wanted us to know that God did what He did for us completely out of the goodness and joy of His heart and without any help from us or even by request from us. We are allowed to enjoy forgiveness, restoration into fellowship with God, and an honored place in His family — all without *having* to do anything or without being *able* to do anything. Even the faith with which we receive Jesus Christ as Lord and Savior is given to us from God.

So what is there for us to boast about in ourselves? Was our resurrection from the dead state of sin into the new life in Christ something we did? Was our salvation something we earned, achieved, accomplished, or purchased? No! The quickening of our spirits was just as much God's workmanship as the resurrection of Jesus! Nothing we did, nor any of our efforts, enabled us to be saved.

No good works.

No serving on this committee or that committee.

No helping out this person or that person.

No denying ourselves this or becoming a member of that.

The workmanship of our new life in Christ was and is completely the workmanship of God.

Let's go back to Abraham, the father of our faith. A very interesting thing happened when God made covenant with Abram in Genesis, chapter 15 — Abram slept right through the entire thing! He had obeyed God by slaying the designated animals and cutting some of them in two pieces, then spent the rest of the day shooing the buzzards away from the carcasses. Finally, as night fell, he went into a deep sleep. By the time the smoking furnace of God passed between the pieces, signifying the covenant, Abram was snoring away!

Grace means: The whole Christian life is not about us; it is the gift of God! It is not about us or our works. Spiritually speaking, it is as though we just kick back, take a nap, and allow God to be God. He then saves us, delivers us, and makes us free forevermore. We have nothing to boast about in ourselves; we only boast in the Lord and what He's done for us. David understood this when he said,

> **I** *will bless the Lord at all times: his praise shall continually be in my mouth.*
> *My soul shall make her boast in the Lord: the humble shall hear thereof, and be glad.*
> *O magnify the Lord with me, and let us exalt his name together.*
>
> PSALM 34:1-3

GRACE IS NOW

In the last chapter, we briefly discussed "for by grace ye are saved," which is found in Ephesians 2:5. We learned that the Holy Spirit was telling us that we were saved at a point in time in our past, but our salvation continues in the present. Now let's look at this concept in more detail.

Paul weaves the fabric of this grace cloth so intricately, even the words he uses are a blessing.

71

The word "saved" comes from the Greek word *sozo*. In Ephesians 2:5, however, it is in a form that begs us to explore it. The word "saved" is in the perfect tense. It means that the action of the verb occurred in the past and the results linger in the present. Paul is saying that our salvation was accomplished in the past and we now exist as saved in the present. If we were to translate this passage with the grammar in mind, it would read:

> **B**y grace have you been saved completely in past time, with the present result that you are in a state of salvation which persists through the present time.
>
> EPHESIANS 2:5 WUEST

This understanding of grace gives our salvation three primary components. **Justification** is the declaration of God that our guilt and the penalty associated with our sin has been revoked and we are placed in a position of right standing with God. **Sanctification** is the outworking of the internal reality that we are separated from the world and now citizens of heaven, God's eternal work within us. Through time and process, God helps us to develop a lifestyle that embraces a holy manner of living. **Glorification** is the full transformation of our bodies into resurrected, immortal bodies. Until then, we will manifest the divine nature of God that has been imparted into our spirit, apprehends our will, and finally, in one grand finale, will one day transform our vile bodies into ones like Jesus' own.

These three words give us a full description of God's grace toward us: We were justified the moment we received Jesus Christ as Lord and Savior; we are being sanctified while we live on this earth; and we will be glorified in the future. Each one of these aspects of our salvation displays God's workmanship in our lives, but the area we are most concerned with right now is, of course, the ongoing work of sanctification. Sanctification is the process of becoming like Jesus, of growing in God. If we are to grow in God, we must grow in grace.

For we are his workmanship, created in Christ Jesus unto good works, which God hath before ordained that we should walk in them.

EPHESIANS 2:10

The word "workmanship" means simply "something that is made." As we have stated emphatically in the introduction, God makes us. We do not make ourselves. Our becoming who we were created to be is the full manifestation of His grace in our everyday lives. There will never come a day when God stops pouring His grace into us. Believers grow from grace to grace and from glory to glory!

God's workmanship in sanctification is working to the outside what He has deposited on the inside.

We have seen how we received everything we could ever want or desire — all spiritual blessings — at the point of the new birth. When we were quickened and made alive in Christ, we were raised and seated with Him in the heavenlies, receiving our eternal identity and purpose. Now Ephesians 2:10 is telling us the same thing in a more practical way. We were created in Christ Jesus to perform good works.

"Good works" does not mean running around helping little old ladies across the street, doling out soup at the homeless shelter once a week, and doing anything that looks like a good deed. "Good works" are God-ordained works, works God prepared for us to walk in. In other words, just as He called us out from before the foundation of the world to be His adopted children, He set the paths in which we would walk and the accomplishments we would achieve.

This is why it is so important to listen to God at all times! When you come to the street corner and notice the little old lady standing next to you, if you have peace in your heart, by all means ask her if she needs some help and give her some assistance if she says yes. Because you are listening to God, He will give you a yank in your spirit if you are not to go near her!

What I am stressing here is that a principle of the kingdom we all must live by is that Jesus ministered according to the leading of the Holy Spirit, not according to the needs of the people. You can rest in the fact that if you have no desire or thought to volunteer at the homeless shelter, but you do have a desire to teach the five-year-olds in Sunday school, stay away from the homeless shelter and sign up to teach! Listen to the leading of the Holy Spirit, not to the need of the moment. This is how you discover and know confidently the works God has prepared for you to walk in.

You cannot walk in your best friend's works. You cannot do the same good works your pastor is doing or the teacher on Christian television is doing. You must walk in the works God has prepared for *you* to walk in. They are your unique, individual works, and they were designed specifically for your personality, your gifts, and your abilities. Again we see how God's workmanship in our lives cries to us, "Be yourself! Be who I made you to be, and do the works I've prepared especially for you."

ENDURING GRACE

For we are his workmanship, created in Christ Jesus unto good works, which God hath before ordained that we should walk in them.

EPHESIANS 2:10

"That we should walk in them" is an interesting phrase. "Walk" is the word *peripateo*, which means "to regulate one's life, to conduct one's self, to order one's behavior." Followed by "in them," the Greek construction is literally saying that we should order our lives within the sphere of the works God has destined us to perform, and there is no way to accomplish this but through the grace of God.

The grace of God is the glue which holds this whole scenario together, for it is the grace of God which saves us, supplies the works in which we are to order our lives, and then gives us the ability to do them! In the same way we relied on the miraculous, saving grace of God to quicken our dead spirit and make us alive spiritually, we must continue to rely on this same miraculous, saving grace to walk in the works He has prepared for us.

We are now talking about the workmanship of God as enduring grace, motivating grace, and persevering grace. Through the grace of God, we frail human beings become superhuman vessels through which the power of God can flow to the world! Remember Paul's thorn in the flesh? Regardless of what you believe that thorn to be, the Bible makes it clear that God's grace is sufficient to see us through any attack, trial, temptation, or grievance that would come our way.

Grace is what God gives us to endure circumstances that often do not change. It is that unchanging, unfailing grace that enabled my wife and me to endure long periods of pain as she recovered from a car accident. For months, I watched as she struggled with pain and depression, unable to walk for a prolonged period of time, and finally just stumbling across the floor of our home.

The accident was sudden and violent. My head hit the windshield and I had some cuts and bruises. My mother-in-law was shaken but okay in the backseat with our two-year-old twins, who in their innocence were exhilarated by this unusual adventure. I kept telling Serita to get out of the car, and she kept saying, "I can't." As I lifted her from the front passenger seat, she cried with pain and my heart sank. Her foot had been crushed by the impact, and I could see a bone piercing through the skin.

This was a tragic injury for both of us. Our hearts and hopes were as crushed as Serita's foot. As a young man filled with hope for the future, intoxicated with the elixir of freshly taken vows, and a passionate lover of his new bride, my ears stung at the doctor's words, "She'll never walk again." My lover, my partner, bone of my bone and flesh of my flesh, had been cruelly crippled. The doctor said that there was an outside chance she would walk with a metal brace, but I was heartbroken.

One never knows from day to day what we will have to face. I tried to look encouraging for her, but I was shaken by the doctor's sobering words. I left the hospital feeling drained and exhausted inside and outside, then tried to explain to my twin sons, who were in diapers, why I had not succeeded in bringing Momma home.

When Serita did come home, she was in a great deal of pain. She struggled to take care of her family despite the constant misery in which she was living. Then came the day she tried to walk for the first time since the accident. She lurched and her foot hit the floor with a thud, her entire body in a twisted, contorted distortion of the once graceful, feminine stride I loved so dearly. I tried to make sure that she never saw the tears that betrayed my confident words of hope and encouragement to her. I suppressed my own pain to undergird her as she warred against her pain and suffering.

Inch by inch and then foot by foot she moved forward as I supported her with my body, soul, and spirit. For a year we persevered through relentless lurching and faltering, with me standing there coaxing and coaching her to continue the fight and believe she would walk again. Then gradually we began to see her gain the slightest trace of strength, then more strength, and finally she began to move normally again.

How did we make it through the long periods of watching her failing miserably, but insisting on taking care of her family? How did Serita stand the unmerciful pain minute by minute and hour by hour and day after day? How did we handle that day when I came home from work to find the love of my life sitting in front of her closet, gazing through tears at the beautiful high-heeled shoes she thought she would never wear again?

It was grace.

It was grace that enabled Serita to walk again. It was grace that caused us to grow up and go up and get stronger and better than ever. It was grace that encouraged us to survive the struggles before us, to endure and overcome pain and grief and fear as we faced the possibility of her never walking again.

Grace is not only a miracle-worker; it is a comfort and strength when miracles are delayed.

No matter how devastating the day may be, we can always expect God's enduring grace to be the undergirding force that keeps our mind from cracking and our feet from falling. Whether our test is our child, our finances, or some other dilemma, when God doesn't alleviate the problem, He gives you the grace to endure the process as you trust Him for your deliverance.

Do you see that this is exactly what the world is looking for? They are looking for the way to endure and persevere so they can achieve their dreams. They are looking for the way to get free and stay free. They are desperate for the ability to live in peace and harmony with other human beings. They are looking for a way to grab hold of eternity and live as though they would never die. The exciting truth is that what I have just described to you is a picture of God's workmanship of grace in the believer today.

Through God's grace, believers can get free and stay free. Through God's grace, believers can live in peace and harmony with other human beings. More importantly, believers can be the living, vital, effective, and productive body of Christ. Through God's grace, believers live as though they would never die because they are alive forever unto God. They can easily give their time, energy, talents, and even their lives because they live in the reality that they are eternal beings.

God graced us with eternal life when we were born again, and one day He will grace us with a glorified, resurrected body like Jesus'. But in the meantime, we have the incredible adventure of appropriating His grace to become more and more like Jesus, to walk out the destiny He has set for us, and to be a light in this dark world.

5

HE BROUGHT US NEAR

Before we were born again and quickened by the Holy Spirit, there was a shroud covering us. This sinister shroud of death and darkness kept us from realizing what we were doing and the consequences of our actions. Essentially, we went about our daily activities oblivious to what was happening in the spirit realm. Then when we were saved and made alive in our spirits, we experienced an unveiling. Suddenly we emerged out of darkness into marvelous light, and that light revealed to us the precarious position we once occupied.

We looked back and saw how far we had been from God.

Part of God's workmanship in our lives and one of the great blessings that comes with salvation is the ability to accurately view our former existence. It is much like a person waking up in their car the morning after a drinking binge. Still experiencing the alcohol-induced amnesia, they open the car door, thinking they are parked safely on the side of the road. Only after they get out of the car and look back do they realize, now enjoying the light of day, that their car is resting on the edge of a cliff! Just one more foot of forward motion and they would have plunged to their death. In a similar fashion, believers are allowed to look back and discover just how close they came to eternal destruction.

> **W**herefore remember, that ye being in time past Gentiles in the flesh, who are called Uncircumcision by that which is called the Circumcision in the flesh made by hands;
> That at that time ye were without Christ, being aliens from the commonwealth of Israel, and strangers from the covenants of promise, having no hope, and without God in the world.
>
> EPHESIANS 2:11-12

Paul ushers us into a time of historical reflection by saying, "Remember, or pull off the shelf, the facts of your past." He wants to display the grace of God on the canvas of the Ephesians' former lives by revealing yet another aspect of their spiritually dead state: As Gentiles, they were the "Uncircumcision."

THE UNCIRCUMCISION

The term "circumcision" can only be called vivid imagery! It refers to a uniquely Jewish practice commanded by God in the Old Testament and was used by God to remind Israel of their covenant with Him. Dealing with the most private and sensitive part of the male body, circumcision symbolized that God desired His people to be honest and forthright with Him in all areas of their lives. He did not want them to hide anything from Him.

In as gentle a way as possible, I will explain what circumcision is. The Bible calls it the cutting away of the flesh, in this case the foreskin from the male organ. It was a surgical procedure that baby boys underwent at eight days old. In the natural, physical world, circumcision is hygienic and helps to prevent infection and disease. In the spiritual sense, the removal of excess tissue from the male private part, the most sensitive area, symbolizes removing the cover from sinful practices. When we lift the cover of pride, expose our sin, and bring it to God, not only does He forgive and cleanse us, but He becomes the source of our lives and our most intimate confidant. In essence, circumcision represents a commitment to living a holy, consecrated life for God.

In his book to the Romans, Paul tells us that when we are born again, we are circumcised in our hearts. When we surrender to Jesus Christ as our Lord and Savior, we are literally removing pride from the most sensitive area of our lives, acknowledging the dilemma regarding our sin, and allowing God to forgive us and give us a new heart. (See Romans 2:29.) So after we are quickened and made alive by the Holy Spirit, we see how the shroud of pride that covered our sin is now lifted and, as Paul instructed us, we look back and understand for the first time how very lost we were.

Although physical circumcision was to be a sign of the covenant God had with the descendants of Abraham, it very soon became a badge of honor or a religious ritual and nothing more. Israel took pride in the fact that circumcision distinguished them from other nations who generally did not practice it, and that pride covered their sin again. Nevertheless, when Paul introduced the Gentiles to the ritual of circumcision in Ephesians, chapter 2, he pointed out the fact that this had been a distinct line of demarcation between Jews and Gentiles.

> **W**herefore remember, that ye being in time past Gentiles in the flesh, who are called Uncircumcision by that which is called the Circumcision in the flesh made by hands;
> That at that time ye were without Christ, being aliens from the commonwealth of Israel, and strangers from the covenants of promise, having no hope, and without God in the world.
>
> EPHESIANS 2:11-12

Literally, being the Uncircumcision meant the Gentiles were cut off from God and His kingdom. When pride rules our heart as a shroud of spiritual death and our spirit is independent from God's Spirit, we live under the following conditions:

Without Christ. We must understand that the word "Christ" in this verse represented the Messiah of Israel, the one whom Israel looked to for deliverance, who would establish them as a prosperous and peaceful nation in the world. God had promised to send a deliverer to the circumcised. Therefore, being "without Christ" meant that the Uncircumcision were without a deliverer. They had no messiah to look for.

Aliens from the commonwealth of Israel. Personally, I love this word, "alien," especially because of its connotation in our time. The term "alien" today carries the meaning of someone from another planet. Similarly, in the biblical sense, "alien" meant someone who was not a citizen, an outsider who was not "at home." The Uncircumcision were excluded from citizenship in Israel as a theocratic nation under the one true God. They were far, far away from God and all He had to offer.

Strangers from the covenants of promise. In the Greek text, this phrase actually reads, "strangers from the covenants of *the* promise." In this particular case, *the* promise referred to is God's promise to send the Messiah to deliver Israel. The Uncircumcision did not have an opportunity to participate in a covenant relationship with God, and therefore they had no promise to insure their future.

Having no hope. Being without hope is being without a future, for how can we face the future without hope? The hope of Israel has always been the Messiah. Therefore, the Uncircumcision looked to a future without hope, for they were not given the promise of the Messiah.

Without God in the world. The Uncircumcision lived in this world without God, literally "apart from God." They had no knowledge of Him or relationship with Him. In this world, they were on their own.

How did this all come about? How did Gentiles get into such a precarious position, existing so far from God? The answer is to be found in the Bible's history of mankind.

THE ORIGIN OF JEW AND GENTILE

In the beginning God created Adam and Eve, who enjoyed the communion of God until they sinned. Because of their sin, God expelled them from the Garden of Eden and they were left to live in a cold and cruel world. Made to work by the sweat of their brow, they produced sons and daughters, and the sin nature began to manifest immediately. Their son Cain slew his brother Abel. Cain was punished, branded, and banished for his actions. Adam and Eve then produced Seth. At this point we have two lines formed, the family of Seth and the family of Cain.

Neither the Cain line nor the Seth line produced godly people. Eventually mankind was so depraved and far from God that God decided to destroy man. Only Noah and his immediate family found grace in the eyes of the Lord. So God had Noah build the ark, collect male and female of every animal, and then He flooded the earth. When the earth was cleansed of all evil people, God set a rainbow in the heaven as a covenant that He would never destroy the earth by water again.

Noah emerged from the ark, planted a vineyard, harvested the grapes, made some wine, and promptly got drunk. One of his grandsons "uncovered his nakedness" (performed a sexual act with Noah) while he was passed out, and the human race was off and running in sin again. The Bible declares that the whole world continued to engage in lawlessness on a massive scale. However, God's promise was unshakable. He would never again destroy the earth with water. Instead, He focused

His attention on a young man named Abram, the son of an idol maker in Ur of the Chaldees.

Because Abram had a heart that could be touched by God, God made a covenant, or drew up a contract, with him. This covenant established that God would use the life and lineage of Abram to produce a nation of godly people. To establish this covenant, God changed Abram's name, which meant "father," to Abraham, which meant "father of a multitude." With this action, God seemed to turn His attention from mankind in general to focus on Abraham and his lineage. He in no way abandoned all of humanity, but intended to use Abraham and his posterity as a tool for evangelizing the whole world. The idea was that God would be so good to Abraham and his descendants, the rest of the world would see His goodness and want God to be their God too.

Out of the loins of this Gentile man named Abram, God started the Hebrew nation. And for the first time in history, the nations were divided by God into two major categories: Jew and Gentile. The Jews were those who had a covenant with God; the Gentiles were the people with no covenant with God. The Jews began to call on God — the invisible one — Elohim, El Shaddai, Almighty God, while the Gentiles worshipped water and fire and Zeus and Aphrodite and birds and trees. God revealed himself to Abraham and to his descendants, becoming known through the centuries as the God of Abraham, Isaac, and Jacob. Unlike the Gentile nations, the nation of Israel was a theocracy, a God-ruled nation.

LINE OF THE MESSIAH

The Jewish line was established when Abraham had Isaac, and Isaac had Jacob, who was renamed Israel, which means "he will rule as God." Again, God indicated He had chosen a people for Himself who had the opportunity and capacity to rule the nations by His power and Word. The nation of Israel was to bring the light of God to the world. Exodus 19:6 states that Israel was ordained to be a kingdom of priests and a holy nation. Unfortunately, the Bible records how Israel repeatedly went from devotion to apathy to outright rebellion with regard to God. Then, when their rebellion led to their near destruction, they would turn back to God and He would deliver them from their enemies. This was a cycle they repeated over and over again through the centuries.

Nevertheless, God would bring His Messiah from the line of the Circumcision. From Israel the man (Jacob) came Israel the nation. Jacob had twelve sons, whose families later became known as the twelve tribes of Israel. The nation of Israel fell into bondage to Egypt for four hundred years, until God sent Moses to deliver them. They walked through the Red Sea on dry land, Pharaoh's army being destroyed behind them, and began their journey back to the land God had given to them.

During the forty-year trek through the wilderness, God preserved them and provided for them supernaturally in the treacherous desert. A pillar of fire by night kept them warm and a pillar of cloud by day kept them cool. Manna dropped from heaven every morning to feed them, and quail were sent when they complained about the manna. Several times water was made available to them by God's miraculous intervention. They were kept healthy and their clothes and shoes didn't wear out. But during this time, God gave the Jewish people something far more precious. He delivered to them what the book of Romans calls the "Oracles of God."

God gave Israel His Law — the principles of His kingdom. He also began to reveal to them His glorious plan of salvation through the form and function of the Tabernacle. There were three parts to the Tabernacle: the outer court, the inner court, and the holy of holies. In each of these sections, there were specific pieces of furniture which represented our redemption through Jesus Christ, the final destination being the holy of holies, where God's presence resided.

If you looked down upon the Tabernacle from a mountaintop, you would see that it was built in the shape of a cross — long before crucifixion existed. This amazing structure had one objective: to move God's people close to Him. Sadly, it was not long before the meaning and symbolism of the Tabernacle degenerated into a religious system. What should have been a glorious age of salvation and deliverance, Israel showing forth the greatness of their God and preaching the Good News of the Messiah to come, became nothing more than a ritualistic and empty series of ceremonies. The most compelling confession of their condition was penned by the prophet Jeremiah:

> The harvest is past, the summer is ended, and we [Israel] are not saved.
>
> JEREMIAH 8:20

Undaunted, God proceeded with His plan. He had promised Israel a deliverer, a messiah, a promised one who would bring peace and prosperity. And what a promise it was!

> The wolf also shall dwell with the lamb, and the leopard shall lie down with the kid; and the calf and

*the young lion and the fatling together; and a little
child shall lead them.*

I S A I A H 11:6

But *he was wounded for our transgressions, he was
bruised for our iniquities: the chastisement of our peace
was upon him; and with his stripes we are healed.*

*All we like sheep have gone astray; we have turned
every one to his own way; and the Lord hath laid on
him the iniquity of us all.*

I S A I A H 53:5-6

And *I will put a new spirit within you; and I will
take the stony heart out of their flesh, and will give
them an heart of flesh:*

*That they may walk in my statutes, and keep mine
ordinances, and do them: and they shall be my people,
and I will be their God.*

E Z E K I E L 11:19-20

Unfortunately, the Jews only heeded the political prophecies. Their Messiah would make the wolf lie down with the lamb and warring factions to become friends. They did not expect a Messiah who would die for their sin and make it possible for their dead spirits to be quickened and made alive to the heart of God. They were looking for someone who would make them political rulers in the earth. When the Messiah Jesus arrived on the scene, the leaders of the nation of Israel promptly and maliciously rejected Him.

Never mind that Jesus worked miracles right in the midst of them.

Never mind that He was a healing, dead-raising prophet and preacher of the living Word.

Never mind that He preached the kingdom of God and lived a sinless, righteous, holy life before them.

When would He destroy the Roman oppressors and put Israel in power?

Ultimately, however, the leaders of Israel rejected Jesus as their Messiah because He claimed to be God. His intimacy with the Father offended their religious thinking and way of life — and intimacy with the Father always rubs the religious folk the wrong way! The religious leaders wanted to control the people through law and ritual and tradition. They didn't want the Holy Spirit telling people what to do!

THE BLOOD OF JESUS

Now we see that God has the mess of the ages on His hands. He looks upon a dispossessed Gentile population, the Uncircumcision, who are aliens from the commonwealth of Israel, strangers to the covenants of promise, and have no hope. And the nation with whom He is in covenant, to whom He gave the Law, the sacrifices, the ordinances of worship, divine favor, and the promise of Messiah, have rejected their own Messiah.

The Gentiles were far from God and didn't even know Him.

The Jews were near — oh so near! — but didn't accept their Deliverer.

> **B**ut now in Christ Jesus ye who sometimes were far off are made nigh by the blood of Christ.
>
> EPHESIANS 2:13

Here we see God's workmanship in bringing the Gentiles to equality with Israel. In verse 12 the Gentiles were without Christ, which referred specifically to the Messiah of Israel. But in verse 13, the name Jesus is added, because through the blood of Jesus of Nazareth, the Uncircumcision "are made nigh"! In the past, the Gentiles had no right to be near God or expect a deliverer, but when Jesus shed His blood on the cross, He brought them near. In verse 14, Paul tells us that Jesus destroyed the wall between Jew and Gentile and made clear that the way of salvation was open to all people.

> **F**or he is our peace, who hath made both one, and hath broken down the middle wall of partition between us.
>
> EPHESIANS 2:14

When Jesus died on the cross as the sacrifice for the sins of mankind, the separation that had existed between God and man since Adam and Eve sinned in the Garden of Eden was destroyed. Man could again be in relationship with God directly through believing in and receiving Christ Jesus as Savior. But these verses of Scripture also tell us that Jesus brought Jew and Gentile to equal footing. Now the human race is not classified as Jew or Gentile, but as believer or unbeliever.

If you are a Jew, your Messiah has come and His name is Jesus of Nazareth. If you are a Gentile, the blood of Jesus Christ has now brought you near. You are no longer an alien, a stranger, without the hope of a deliverer. Jesus has broken down the wall between Jew and Gentile and has made both one, calling them all and drawing them all into His body, the Church. We must all come to God the same way, through Christ Jesus.

Although many Jews believed on Jesus and were saved, later becoming part of the first century Church, Israel as a nation rejected Jesus as Messiah. Eventually, the Church was predominantly Gentiles. Lest we Gentiles begin to be puffed up with pride, in Ephesians 2, the apostle Paul commands us to look back to the cross and remember that at one time we were afar off and so despicably lost and depraved that we were literally looked upon as dogs. Thank God, Jesus doesn't call the Gentiles dogs anymore!

> **B**ut now in Christ Jesus ye who sometimes were far off are made nigh by the blood of Christ.
>
> EPHESIANS 2:13

What a glorious time to live! Gentiles are near and Jews have their promise fulfilled, which means all of us have the promise of the Deliverer. The war between us is over! No longer do we squabble and fight over circumcision and washings and feast days and sacrifices — Jesus has fulfilled them all. Through the blood of Jesus Christ, *all* of us are brought nigh to God!

6

HE IS
OUR PEACE

For he is our peace, who hath made both one, and hath broken down the middle wall of partition between us.

EPHESIANS 2:14

Jesus *is* our peace.

The Bible does not say that He gives us peace or that He sends us peace. He *is* our peace. This is wonderful! That means when we have Him, we have peace. When He becomes our Lord and Savior, peace is ours forever, no matter what situation we find ourselves in. If they put us in jail it doesn't matter, because He is our peace. If they exile us to the desert it is all right, because He is our peace. We don't get peace from the things He gives us, but from His presence in our lives.

Aside from the Holy Spirit shedding the love of God abroad in our hearts, obtaining His peace that passes all understanding is one of the greatest gifts of God's workmanship in our lives. This is an incredible blessing! Wherever we go and whatever we are doing, we have peace! This work of peace encompasses, enriches, and enhances so many areas of our lives. And it all happened when Jesus destroyed that which caused enmity between God and mankind, and Jew and Gentile.

ABOLISHING ENMITY

Having abolished in his flesh the enmity, even the law of commandments contained in ordinances; for to make in himself of twain one new man, so making peace.

EPHESIANS 2:15

The word "abolished" means "to cease or to make of no effect." When Jesus died on the cross, He stopped the law and made it ineffectual. The word "enmity" indicates great hostility, likened unto war or extreme conflict. The apostle Paul gives us the root cause of this hostility: the law. You see, the Jewish law was more than just the Ten Commandments. It was "even the law of commandments contained in ordinances." This phrase, first of all, refers to the myriad of laws pertaining to everything from adultery to agriculture. If you have never read through your entire Bible, then you will probably not have read Exodus, Leviticus, Numbers, and Deuteronomy, the books where all of these judgments and ordinances are given.

The Ten Commandments were the first presentation of God's law to Israel and to mankind at large. They were a kind of paramount overview of His will, with the first four commandments relating to man's relationship to God and the last six relating to man's relationship to man. Then there were the dietary, cultural, and relational laws, which enumerated what to eat and what not to eat, when to plant and when to reap, and how to treat your family and your neighbors. The judgments commanded specific punishments for each violation of these laws. Then there were the ordinances, which dealt with how Israel was to present herself to God as an act of worship or to be forgiven for sins committed, both as individuals and as a nation. These laws included how the priests were to present the various offerings of worship and sacrifices for sin, as well as how the ark of the covenant was to be handled.

The nation of Israel took pride not only in the fact that their men were circumcised and they had the hope of a deliverer, their messiah. They were also set apart because God had given them the law. Unlike the Gentile nations, the Jews *knew* what was right and what was wrong because God himself had given the law to Moses. They were experts on the definition of sin, and they were careful not to associate with all the Gentile nations who knew nothing about God or His law.

As a result, the Jews considered the Gentiles unclean and treated them as they would treat lepers. They called them dogs, and in those days, a dog was not a beloved household pet! Being called a dog was a great insult. In every area of life, from the daily activities of living to the major feasts and holy days, the nation of Israel ordered their lives according to the "law of commandments contained in ordinances." Their entire way of life and operation as a nation was different from any other nation on earth, and they had great disdain and contempt for anyone who lived differently. Can you see how the law caused enmity between Jew and Gentile?

Now again, we must remember that this was not God's plan. His purpose in giving the law was to reveal to His people that they were sinners in need of a savior. Paul explains this clearly in his letter to the Galatians:

> **W**herefore the law was our schoolmaster to bring us unto Christ, that we might be justified by faith.
>
> But after that faith is come, we are no longer under a schoolmaster.
>
> For ye are all the children of God by faith in Christ Jesus.
>
> GALATIANS 3:24-26

God presented the law to Israel as the standard which couldn't possibly be met in their present unregenerated, spiritually dead state. To reinforce this concept, He also commanded His people to build the Tabernacle, and later the Temple, not just for a place of worship, but as a place to offer sacrifices for their sins. Every time they sinned as individuals or as a nation, the law stipulated exactly what sacrifice had to be made for that particular sin. Then, once a year on the Day of Atonement, the high priest would sprinkle the blood of a goat upon the mercy seat of the ark of the covenant, the piece of furniture in the holy of holies, and turn a second goat loose to wander in the desert. This annual sacrifice and ritual was the atonement for all of Israel's sin for the year. Most importantly, it was a type and foreshadowing of Jesus' work on the cross.

And he shall take the two goats, and present them before the Lord at the door of the tabernacle of the congregation.

And Aaron shall cast lots upon the two goats; one lot for the Lord, and the other lot for the scapegoat....

Then shall he kill the goat of the sin offering, that is for the people, and bring his blood within the vail, and do with that blood as he did with the blood of the bullock, and sprinkle it upon the mercy seat, and before the mercy seat:

And he shall make an atonement for the holy place, because of the uncleanness of the children of Israel, and because of their transgressions in all their sins: and so shall he do for the tabernacle of the congregation, that remaineth among them in the midst of their uncleanness.

LEVITICUS 16:7-8,15-16

And *when he hath made an end of reconciling the holy place, and the tabernacle of the congregation, and the altar, he shall bring the live goat:*

And Aaron shall lay both his hands upon the head of the live goat, and confess over him all the iniquities of the children of Israel, and all their transgressions in all their sins, putting them upon the head of the goat, and shall send him away by the hand of a fit man into the wilderness:

And the goat shall bear upon him all their iniquities unto a land not inhabited: and he shall let go the goat in the wilderness.

LEVITICUS 16:20-22

God commanded that a goat be slain on the Day of Atonement because a goat is the biblical symbol of the sin nature, of man in his most depraved state. You know, a goat will eat anything! It's common to see goats eating garbage and all kinds of filth. Furthermore, goats are very independent and will wander this way and that to eat anything that catches their eye, whereas sheep are dependent upon their shepherd for everything. In the Bible, sheep are a type of the believer and goats are a type of the unbeliever.

104

When Jesus went to the cross, the Bible tells us that He *became* sin that we might *become* righteous. (See 2 Corinthians 5:21.) Jesus became the goat, crucifying our sin nature on the cross to satisfy God's wrath against it. Then, when God was satisfied that our debt had been paid, through Jesus Christ we could then be made righteous.

But why did God command a second goat, a live goat, to be used in this ritual? The high priest, in this case Aaron, laid his hands on the live goat and pronounced all of Israel's sin upon it. Then he banished the goat to wander in the wilderness. Jesus also took our sin to the depths of hell and left it there, where it belongs. He threw our sin right back in the face of the devil himself! Praise God!

You will remember also that when Jesus died on the cross, the veil or large, thick curtain separating the holy place and the holy of holies in the Temple was torn supernaturally from top to bottom. (See Matthew 27:51.) God did that to signify that the final sacrifice had been made for all sin for all time. No more goats were to be sacrificed on the Day of Atonement! No more spotless lambs during Passover! All violations against the law were paid as the blood of Jesus poured to the ground. From that moment on, every believer could be born again, forgiven of their past, present, and future sins, and have the law written in their heart!

> **A**nd I will put a new spirit within you; and I will take the stony heart out of their flesh, and will give them an heart of flesh:
>
> That they may walk in my statutes, and keep mine ordinances, and do them: and they shall be my people, and I will be their God.
>
> EZEKIEL 11:19-20

There is no more enmity and hostility between Jew and Gentile, and there is no more enmity and hostility between God and man because Jesus abolished the law on the cross. The issue today is not keeping the law, and if you don't succeed, making the proper sacrifice at the Temple. The issue today is following the leading of the Holy Spirit. Today, *believers* are the temple of the Holy Ghost! We are living sacrifices unto our God. If we follow the Holy Spirit, we will always stay in God's will and keep His law. God's workmanship has given us peace!

IT'S ALWAYS BEEN FAITH

> **A**nd that he might reconcile both unto God in one body by the cross, having slain the enmity thereby.
>
> EPHESIANS 2:16

Paul changes directions in verse 16 because the enmity being slain on the cross here is not the hostility between Jew and Gentile, but the hostility between all mankind and God. Although God had made covenant with the Jews, and they were considered near to God, the Jews needed to be born again as much as the Gentiles. When a Jew is born again, they become a part of the new body, the Church, just as the Gentiles do.

And came and preached peace to you which were afar off, and to them that were nigh.

EPHESIANS 2:17

Jesus preached peace to "you which were afar off" (Paul is referring to the Ephesians, who were Gentiles), "and to them that were nigh" (the Jews). He went first to the house of Israel in His three years of ministry, because the Jews were near to God. What we are seeing in Ephesians 2:11-17 explains a passage of Scripture which many of us don't understand or even want to deal with because it portrays Jesus being uncharacteristically rude and uncompassionate.

And, behold, a woman of Canaan came out of the same coasts, and cried unto him, saying, Have mercy on me, O Lord, thou son of David; my daughter is grievously vexed with a devil.

107

But he answered her not a word. And his disciples came and besought him, saying, Send her away; for she crieth after us.

But he answered and said, I am not sent but unto the lost sheep of the house of Israel.

Then came she and worshipped him, saying, Lord, help me.

But he answered and said, It is not meet to take the children's bread, and to cast it to dogs.

And she said, Truth, Lord: yet the dogs eat of the crumbs which fall from their masters' table.

Then Jesus answered and said unto her, O woman, great is thy faith: be it unto thee even as thou wilt. And her daughter was made whole from that very hour.

MATTHEW 15:22-28

Can you see the enmity that existed between Jew and Gentile? And yet, in the very midst of this hostility and tension, Jesus smashes the law to smithereens and wipes out the enmity with God's grace, mercy, and compassion! He responds to this Gentile woman's faith and even commends her for it. We are struck with the fact that it is truly faith in the Lord Jesus Christ that fulfills all the law! (Read Galatians 3:24-26 again.)

This woman was a Canaanite, and Canaanites were the most depraved of Gentile nations. Even archeologists have found abounding evidence of the rampant and terrible immorality among this people. She was *unclean,* and yet Jesus accepted her!

Why? Because of her faith. She recognized the Deliverer and refused to let go of Him, no matter what it cost her. She didn't care if He called her a dog! She was not moving until He became *her* Lord and healed her daughter.

Of course, the disciples did not understand why Jesus even spoke to the Canaanite woman because they were still so entrenched in the law. They did not catch on to the fact that Jesus was demonstrating salvation by His grace, through faith. Later, when the Jews cried that the law came from God and the law was the way of salvation, the apostle Paul would argue, "You remember your father Abraham? Was he righteous because of the law?"

They would say, "Well, no. Abraham lived before the law was given."

"Well then," Paul would ask, "Was he righteous because he was circumcised?"

"Uh, no. He was justified before God commanded circumcision."

"Okay, I see. Was Abraham a Hebrew then?"

"No, he was a Gentile."

"Yes," Paul would agree, "Abraham was a Gentile who by faith believed God and it was counted unto him as righteousness." (See Romans 4:3.) Abraham became a Jew only when he surrendered his life to God.

For he is not a Jew, which is one outwardly; neither is that circumcision, which is outward in the flesh:

But he is a Jew, which is one inwardly; and circumcision is that of the heart, in the spirit, and not in the letter; whose praise is not of men, but of God.

ROMANS 2:28-29

A NEW WAY

In a practical sense, the "law of commandments contained in ordinances" covered three areas of life. First, it set up the theocracy, the government of God over the nation of Israel. This contained the judgments, which dealt with how the people handled each other. If anyone committed a crime, or there was a conflict between two people, the law told them how the situation should be handled. For example, if your neighbor stole your ox and was caught with the goods, the law commanded your neighbor to return to you twice what he stole.

If the theft be certainly found in his hand alive, whether it be ox, or ass, or sheep; he shall restore double.

EXODUS 22:4

Second, the "law of commandments contained in ordinances" commanded what sacrifices were to be offered for what sins, also commanding various washings, cleansings, and absolutions. Essentially, these were outward practices which symbolized the forgiveness and cleansing of sins committed. The following verse tells a person how to wash themselves if they eat something that is unclean.

> **A**nd every soul that eateth that which died of itself, or that which was torn with beasts, whether it be one of your own country, or a stranger, he shall both wash his clothes, and bathe himself in water, and be unclean until the even: then shall he be clean.
>
> LEVITICUS 17:15

Third, the law dealt with how to worship. There were specific feasts (Feast of Tabernacles, Feast of Unleavened Bread, Feast of the Firstfruits, for example) and holy days, such as the days of Purim (remembering Queen Esther's act of courage to save Israel from destruction) and the Day of Atonement, which we have already described. Then there were various offerings, such as peace offerings, drink offerings, and heave offerings. These were to remind the children of Israel that the source of all wealth and prosperity was the Lord.

> **A**nd the Lord spake unto Moses, saying,
> Speak unto the children of Israel, and say unto them, When ye come into the land whither I bring you,
> Then it shall be, that, when ye eat of the bread of the land, ye shall offer up an heave offering unto the Lord.

Ye shall offer up a cake of the first of your dough for an heave offering: as ye do the heave offering of the threshingfloor, so shall ye heave it.

NUMBERS 15:17-20

Now, I don't know about you, but all these laws and judgments and ordinances do not sound like a life of peace to me! Being consumed with the law and ordinances and washings and sacrifices and offerings does not bring peace, but is a constant reminder of the enmity and conflict between God and man. God is righteous and man is not, so for the two to have any kind of relationship, man must continually be washing and cleansing and working, working, working to keep God satisfied.

How would you like to wake up every morning and go to bed every night studying the law to make certain you hadn't broken any of it? Then, if you had broken a law, you would have to find out what you needed to do to be made clean. Can you see yourself on Saturday night, running all over town trying to find the perfect goat to sacrifice at the altar the next morning?

And if any one of the common people sin through ignorance, while he doeth somewhat against any of the commandments of the Lord concerning things which ought not to be done, and be guilty;

Or if his sin, which he hath sinned, come to his knowledge: then he shall bring his offering, a kid of the goats, a female without blemish, for his sin which he hath sinned.

And he shall lay his hand upon the head of the sin offering, and slay the sin offering in the place of the burnt offering.

LEVITICUS 4:27-29

How would you like a church service like that? Thank God, Jesus fulfilled and abolished all of the law and the sacrifices! Now we have peace because He is the ultimate, final sacrifice and our complete redemption from sin. He is our feast of unleavened bread. He is our passover lamb. He is our drink offering and our wave offering. Do you understand what I'm saying to you?

Jesus is our Sabbath, and when we come to Him we have entered into complete and total rest. He is our scapegoat, and because of Him our sins have been carried into the wilderness and forgotten forever! The wine that we drink represents His blood, and the bruising of His body is our health and healing. His flesh is the veil in the Temple rent from the top to the bottom, and He is our peace!

Jesus is the fulfillment of everything the Old Testament law and ordinances foreshadowed. He is the concrete reality of every abstraction found in the Tabernacle and Temple design and furniture. When we receive Jesus, God's workmanship in our hearts sees that we keep the Sabbath holy. In fact, we keep every day holy!

> **S**urely his salvation is nigh them that fear him; that glory may dwell in our land.
>
> Mercy and truth are met together; righteousness and peace have kissed each other.
>
> Truth shall spring out of the earth; and righteousness shall look down from heaven.
>
> Yea, the Lord shall give that which is good; and our land shall yield her increase.
>
> Righteousness shall go before him; and shall set us in the way of his steps.
>
> PSALM 85:9-13

God opened David's eyes and he looked through time to see Jesus bringing mercy and truth together. He saw righteousness and peace in one. He saw the fulfillment of the law in his Messiah. He saw that in Christ Jesus were all blessing and honor and glory and power! David was looking at a new thing that was based purely on faith in Jesus Christ. He saw us, the Church, enjoying peace with God through the blood of Jesus.

Whether Jew or Gentile, God's workmanship has made peace available to all men, women, and children on the earth through Jesus Christ. Eternal, unfathomable, life-transforming peace comes from simply being in right relationship with God, and that is what Jesus' death and resurrection offers us.

Peace is knowing Jesus as our Lord and Savior. Peace is being quickened and made alive in our spirits. And this is not a peace that disappears on us when life starts spinning in chaos and confusion or the bottom drops out from beneath us! Yes, when storms come we will feel them strike our flesh and we may even experience some fear, but on the inside of us we have a peace that passes all understanding.

Jesus *is* our peace, and He will never leave us nor forsake us.

The apostle Paul was God's appointed steward of the revelation of grace, but he was also intensely preoccupied with building the Church. The more I study about him, the more I'm fascinated because he was a Hebrew man whom God called to minister to Gentiles. Before he was born again his Hebrew name was Saul, reminiscent of the fact that he came from the lineage of the tribe of Benjamin, because the first king of Israel was also named Saul, a Benjamite. But Paul was also a citizen of Rome, which brought many privileges. So today we would say that he was multicultural. Wherever he went, he would adapt to the culture and customs and language of the people he was with in order to win them to Christ.

> **G**ive none offence, neither to the Jews, nor to the Gentiles, nor to the church of God:

Even as I please all men in all things, not seeking mine own profit, but the profit of many, that they may be saved.

1 CORINTHIANS 10:32-33

There is no doubt that Paul had one of the deepest understandings of God's vision of the maturing, increasing, growing Church. More than any other, he expounded on the coming together of Jew and Gentile and the one way of salvation through Jesus Christ, which was open to all mankind.

HEAVENLY ACCESS

A wonderful reality sets in when we realize that we all have access to God through Jesus Christ.

For through him we both have access by one Spirit unto the Father.

EPHESIANS 2:18

The word "access" is the Greek word *prosagoogeen*, which has a very rich meaning in antiquity. This word depicts a formal entree into the presence of a king or deity, a "royal audience," so to speak. Furthermore, it also denotes a confidence and boldness to enter the presence of that dignitary. The book of Hebrews expresses it perfectly:

Let us therefore come boldly unto the throne of grace, that we may obtain mercy, and find grace to help in time of need.

Being in Christ gives us the position and legal right to enter the heavenly throne room, but the Holy Spirit who lives inside us is the one who ushers us into the presence of God with confidence and boldness. We all have access by one Spirit, our Comforter, our Teacher, our Guide. He is in all of us and His job is to unite us with the Father and unite us with one another.

We are *commanded* by the Word of God to come boldly into the throne room of God to obtain mercy and grace in our time of need. This is an awesome, mind-boggling privilege! Moreover, in the context in which Paul is speaking to us in Ephesians, he is saying that even though I come from generations of heathens, I have just as much access to the Father as the Jew who has known and served Him for centuries!

Whether we are black, brown, white, yellow, or red, we now have access to the Father's house! How do you get in your house? You have access. If you didn't have access, you couldn't get in. You must understand what Paul is saying here. *All* of us heathens were wrong. The black man was doing something crazy in Africa, the white man was doing something crazy in Europe, the yellow man was doing something crazy in China, the brown man was doing something crazy in South America, and the red man was doing something crazy in North America — and God just snatched all of us out with the glorious Gospel of Jesus Christ and gave us all access. He looked us straight in the eye, pointed to His Son, Jesus, and said, "Here's your key — your access — into My house. Please come." Thank You, Lord!

Let me give you a practical, everyday example of the power and peace found in the fact that we have access into the heavenly realm. Do you remember on the Sea of Galilee, when the storm was raging, the disciples were about to drown, and Jesus was asleep at the back of the boat? (See Mark 4:35-41.) The lightning was flashing and the thunder was roaring and the ship was tossing to and fro...*when Peter spoke to Jesus.* And when Peter spoke to Jesus, his words did something that the storm couldn't do. Peter's words awoke Jesus!

The storms of life don't disturb God or incite His compassion to move in our behalf — we do! He is listening for the voices of His children who call on His name in faith. When we open our mouths, address Him as Father, and come in the name of Jesus, we have access to Him. We are immediately present with Him in His throne room of mercy and grace.

We don't have access to just part of Him.

We don't have access for a limited time.

The fullness of God is made available to us and is present with us forever, whenever we call upon His name. Our access is an eternal fact! It is proof positive that we have been raised and are now seated with Jesus in heaven. Our Heavenly Father expects us to come into His house and into His presence confidently and boldly.

There is no "access denied" when we pray.

There is no "limited availability" clause.

There is no "except in certain cases" rule.

There are no "time limits" in the contract.

We have eternal access to the presence of God with no geographic limitations. We can be in a gymnasium, but we have access to the presence of God. How can this be? Because we *are* the house of God, the dwelling place of His presence. The precious Holy Spirit dwells in us. Wherever we are, that place can be filled with the glory of God and become His sanctuary because we bear His presence inside of us at all times and in all places.

Are you enjoying to its fullest capacity the privilege you have to access God at will? Do you recognize that the angels of the Lord are encamped around you and that the presence of God is nearer than your own breath?

WE'RE IN THE HOUSE!

Now therefore ye are no more strangers and foreigners, but fellowcitizens with the saints, and of the household of God.

EPHESIANS 2:19

We are no longer strangers and foreigners. No more! We are part of the family and household of God, and in this verse He pronounces a benediction on us. He tells us to stop bringing up our past because we are no longer strangers and foreigners, but members of His family. We have access to Him and His home, and we are to "come home" confidently and boldly at all times and in all places and under all circumstances. If we approach God like a foreigner, we approach Him in unbelief, timidly crying and begging, "I hope You don't run me out. Please let me in." And God will stare at us incredulously, wondering, *What's wrong with you?*

What would you think if one of your children came to your house like that? Wouldn't you think it ludicrous if you were in your house and one of your kids came up to the front door and started ringing the doorbell? You'd say, "What's wrong with you? You know you don't have to ring the doorbell. You live here. You're not one of the neighbors who live in another house. You're not a stranger from across town. You're not a foreigner who is just visiting from another country. You are my child, my flesh and blood!"

So God is standing there with His arms folded, saying, "What are you doing ringing the bell when Jesus died to give you the key? You can come in and out and find green pastures whenever you want. You're one of My kids now. My Spirit dwells in your spirit, and I have drawn you near to Me, to live in My house forever."

"I know," you say, "but you don't know what I've been going through." You are into your conditions again and have forgotten your position! If you ever get a grip on your position — that you are of the household of God, living in His miracle-producing, peace-inducing presence — you're going to break through your conditions! You're no more a stranger! You're no more a foreigner! You are a fellow citizen with the saints of the household of God. God's workmanship has placed you in His house!

THE BODY IN THREE FORMS

Now therefore ye are no more strangers and foreigners, but fellowcitizens with the saints, and of the household of God;

And are built upon the foundation of the apostles and prophets, Jesus Christ himself being the chief corner stone;

In whom all the building fitly framed together groweth unto an holy temple in the Lord.

EPHESIANS 2:19-21

Paul gives us three illustrations of what the body of Christ is in these verses. First, we are "fellow citizens with the saints." Second, we are "of the household of God." And third, we are a "holy temple in the Lord." As "fellow citizens with the saints," we are citizens of the city of God and of heaven. I'm not certain many of the saints, particularly in America, understand that today. Most of the Church is more in love with the world than they are with who they are in Christ. They are more concerned about what's going on in the earth than what they are supposed to be doing here.

To wit, that God was in Christ, reconciling the world unto himself, not imputing their trespasses unto them; and hath committed unto us the word of reconciliation.

Now then we are ambassadors for Christ, as though God did beseech you by us: we pray you in Christ's stead, be ye reconciled to God.

2 CORINTHIANS 5:19-20

Every believer should remember at all times that they are not of this world, but merely sojourners on this earth and ambassadors for Christ to this world.

Before salvation, we were aliens to God and citizens of earth; after salvation, we are aliens to this world and citizens of heaven. We are not of this world! We are citizens of heaven used by God to preach the Gospel and make disciples of all nations. That is the ministry of reconciliation which all believers have and which Paul reminds us of in these verses.

Then Paul tells us that we are "of the household of God." We have talked a lot about what it means to be a member of God's family, having complete access to His throne room and the privilege of walking in His presence at all times. As His dear children, we can walk, talk, and fellowship with Him continually, all day and all night if we wish. He is our loving Father forever.

It's very hard for me to speak about God being a Father today because so many have had no father in their home. Or, if they did have a father in their home, he was nearly the opposite in character and behavior to our heavenly Father. If you are one of these, don't be afraid to open your heart to God and allow Him to be the father you always hoped existed and yearned with all your heart to know! In the most powerful way, you will see His workmanship of restoration and peace in your life!

Believe me when I say that our Father God is the one you have been dreaming of, who loves you no matter where you've been, what you've done, or who you've been with. You are the child He wanted, and if you have any doubt of His wanting you, look to the cross. That's how much He wanted you! As you let Him love you and heal you, you will become secure in His household and secure in the plan He has for your life.

Finally, Paul says that we are "a holy temple in the Lord." If you think you are excited about being a citizen of heaven and a member of God's family, just wait until you get a glimpse of being His holy temple! Now we are confronted with something that goes even farther beyond our imagination and natural understanding, something magnificent in every sense and concept.

FITLY FRAMED TOGETHER

The Ephesians had built one of the biggest and most elaborate temples ever constructed on the earth — a temple to the pagan goddess Diana. Even today, this temple is considered one of the most incredible edifices of the ancient world. Now Paul is writing to the believers who live in the shadow of that temple, saying, "You are now the temple of the Lord! And you are far more magnificent in beauty, far more masterful in construction, and far more holy than the greatest temple human beings have ever built."

> **A**nd are built upon the foundation of the apostles and prophets, Jesus Christ himself being the chief corner stone;
>
> In whom all the building fitly framed together groweth unto an holy temple in the Lord.
>
> EPHESIANS 2:20-21

To understand God's supernatural construction of this holy temple, we must begin with the foundation, which the Bible tells us is the apostles and prophets. The prophets represent the Old Testament and the apostles represent the New Testament. Paul is saying, "Jesus is the fulfillment of the Old Testament, and the New Testament is the revelation of Him and His body, and both must be treated as the inerrant Word of God."

Our foundation is, was, and always will be God's Word. It is the Word which gives us stability and understanding to stand strong and to be effective in our calling. It is the Word which is the rock of our salvation, the rock which holds us together and empowers us when the storms of life rage against us. It is the Word of God that keeps us from being deceived and wandering off the path God has set for us. It is the Word of God which builds our faith, gives us revelation and understanding, and enables us to carry out God's will for our lives.

Then Paul says, "Jesus Christ himself being the chief corner stone." Who is the Living Word? Who fulfilled the Old Testament prophecies and satisfied every jot and tittle of the law? Who appointed the twelve apostles, continues to appoint the ministry gifts, and places all believers in their callings today? Whose blood abolished the enmity between God and man and Jew and Gentile? That would be our chief cornerstone, the one who holds this building called the Church together.

The term "cornerstone" is significant to the uniting of Jew and Gentile believers and New and Old Testaments because the cornerstone, by definition, brings two walls together. When a building is constructed, a large stone is placed at the corner which will join two walls, usually perpendicular to one another. Each of these walls is going in a different direction and has a specific function, but the cornerstone joins them, and together they form a new building. No longer two separate edifices serving different purposes, they unite to form an entirely new structure, one which has infinitely more space, strength, power, and potential than the walls had by themselves. Do you see the multiplying, unifying, supernatural power of Jesus, the chief cornerstone?

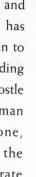

Now that God has laid such an excellent and eternal foundation, with a cornerstone that has stood every stress test known to man, we begin to build upon this firm foundation, "all the building fitly framed together." By "fitly framed," the apostle Paul describes the work of a master craftsman stonecutter who chisels away at each stone, smoothing the rough edges, cutting away the excess, and filling in the holes. The elaborate process of stone cutting makes each stone unique, able to fulfill its particular function and to fit with every stone around it.

> *Ye also, as lively stones, are built up a spiritual house, an holy priesthood, to offer up spiritual sacrifices, acceptable to God by Jesus Christ.*
>
> 1 PETER 2:5

Each of us are lively, or living, stones, and in order for us to fit together, God works on us, continually growing us up and maturing us into the living sacrifice He has ordained us to be. We must also remember that He places believers in every generation and in every nation on that solid foundation so that we are all one building, consisting of the saints who have gone before us and those who will follow us, made up of every race and nationality.

God places this person into place and that person into place, this ministry into place and that ministry into place, this church body into place and that church body into place. Every stone is fitly framed — shaped, molded, and formed — to do its part in the building. Oh, some of us are pretty rough stones when we are brought to the building site! But we're in the hands of the Master, the one who knows just how to chisel and shape us and set us into the building in a way that we fit.

We hear a lot today about independent ministries and independent churches and independent believers. How are you going to be independent in a body? If you tie a finger off from the hand, it dies! If your knees decide to leave and join an army of just knees, your body collapses (and the army of knees is not going to go far either!). Only the body where each part fulfills its function will stand healthy and strong. And, when we truly become fitly framed together, we will be a fortress which the enemy cannot get over, get around, or go through! We will become a habitation in which God is fully present and His glory fills us and flows through us and overflows from us to others.

GROWING IN HOLINESS

In whom all the building fitly framed together groweth unto an holy temple in the Lord.

EPHESIANS 2:21

The Greek language in this verse indicates that this building is continually growing. This building we know as the Church is not made with hands, but of lives fitted together by the Spirit and created for growth. It is created for outreach. It is designed to be continuously "added on to" by the Holy Spirit. Paul writes that we are a giant temple continuously under construction. If we're not growing, we're not healthy, and we're not becoming more holy.

It is very important to know that Paul chose the word *naos* when he spoke of us being a temple, because *naos* is the word used for the inner sanctuary, or the holy of holies, of the Temple of Jerusalem. He did not choose the word *hieros*, which meant the outer courts. The holy of holies is where the ark of the covenant was placed and the presence of God resided. By using this word, Paul is saying, "We are a building which, as we mature and multiply under the direction of the Holy Spirit, will rise up to become a holy place, a place where the presence of God resides at all times."

In the Old Testament, the ark of the covenant was the foremost sign of God's presence. It was kept in the Tabernacle, a temporary tent-like structure. Long gold-covered poles of wood, called staves, were put through rings on each side of the ark so that it could be carried on the shoulders of the priests whenever the ark was moved. The Tabernacle is a picture of the individual believer. We live in "tents," our bodies, as we move through this earth, and the ark, or presence of God, moves with us. God's anointing rests on us, just as the ark rested on the shoulders of the priests who carried it.

But as the Church, corporately we become the Temple, stationary and holy and immovable. No longer are we moving about as tents; we are living stones, fitly framed together and increasing and growing into the holy temple of the Lord. When the ark was placed in the Temple in Jerusalem, the staves were removed from it. It was now in its permanent home! The anointing and glory of God filled the entire Temple, and the cloud of God's presence was so strong that the priests could not stand to minister — they fell prostrate in worship. (See 1 Kings 8:1-11.)

When the Lord sees us come together in corporate worship, He pulls out the staves and says, "I'm staying here in the midst of My people. I will walk up and down in the midst of them. I will pour out My anointing on them and make them a holy people, full of My grace and glory!"

It is at this point that the eternal attributes of God and the *position* we have in Christ Jesus break through and have direct bearing on our *condition*. We become "a holy temple in the Lord." The word "holy" paints a picture of who we are and how we operate. We are consecrated and set apart for God's exclusive use; He alone is the one we follow and serve. We love Him with all of our heart, and when God has our whole heart, He has our whole life. Now we begin to see His workmanship in bringing us into unity and the power of becoming one.

8

HE MADE US ONE

*P*aul was called primarily to minister to the Gentiles, but he had a passion for the Jewish believer and the Gentile believer to understand that they were now one in Christ Jesus. If he were in America, he would perhaps be dealing with black Christians and white Christians because he was on a mission to tear down any kind of division in order to bring unity to the body. Interestingly enough, the first instance of Gentiles coming into the body of Christ did not happen to Paul, but to Peter.

ONE DOOR FOR ALL

In Acts, chapter 10, an unusual and unprecedented event occurred at the house of a Gentile named Cornelius. God had commanded the apostle Peter to go to this man's home and share the Gospel with him. When Peter spoke the truth of Christ Jesus, the Holy Spirit fell on all those who heard him speak, and Peter and the other Jews who were with him were astonished that the gift of the Holy Spirit was poured out on the Gentiles. In this intense and historical moment, the Jew and Gentile came together as one to form the Church — the Holy Spirit united them in the body of Christ.

The Church has only one door, and both Jew and Gentile have to stoop to get in that door. By stoop, I mean they must bow their knees to Jesus and acknowledge Him and Him alone as their Lord. The Jew has to humble himself from legalism and traditions of men and accept the door of faith. The Gentile has to repent of his heathen ways and come in the same door of faith. Jesus said:

> I *am the door: by me if any man enter in, he shall be saved, and shall go in and out, and find pasture.*
>
> John 10:9

When we pass through that door, we are renouncing our allegiance to everything else and joining ourselves to this new workmanship that is created unto Christ Jesus unto good works. The Jew had to go through the door of their Messiah, Jesus, to get in. The Romans also had to go through Jesus to get in. And every nationality on the earth has to enter through this one, solitary door, no matter whether you are male, female, educated, or illiterate. There are no big "I's" or little "yous." There is only one way in and that is through faith in Christ Jesus.

In Ephesians 2:14, the apostle Paul stated that Jesus "hath made both one." This new thing is not a Jewish thing or a Gentile thing. He has made both one as they believe on the Lord Jesus Christ and are saved.

> **T**here is neither Jew nor Greek, there is neither bond nor free, there is neither male nor female: for ye are all one in Christ Jesus.
>
> GALATIANS 3:28

Paul made it clear that in Christ, there is neither male nor female, Greek nor Jew, bond nor free, but all are one if they will confess Jesus Christ as Lord. The Church is to be a meeting ground for both genders, all nationalities, all social levels, all races, and all cultures. The Church is a fusion place. It is a place that has its own ethnicity — the ethnicity of being a royal priesthood, a holy nation, a new people.

God has never cared about differences in skin tones and hair colors and facial features. Only one thing matters to Him: whether we are in covenant relationship with Him. And the only way to be in covenant relationship with Him is through Christ Jesus. God sees only two categories of people: saved and not saved, believers and unbelievers, born again and not born again. Either we know God through Jesus Christ or we don't. Even in the Old Testament,

God did not care if a Jew married a Gentile as long as that Gentile was a believer in Him.

The master will of God is that all things might come together in Christ — divisions might be healed, breaches might be mended, sin might be wiped out, and righteousness might reign. The master will of God is that all things might conform to Jesus Christ and find their wholeness and their fulfillment in Him.

TOGETHER FOREVER

Today, when Paul got through tearing down the walls of racial prejudice, he would then be jumping on denominationalism because his whole mission was to make believers understand that the Church is one entity. When we join it, we pledge allegiance to every single brother and sister who is a part of the body of Christ. We are literally raised up together, not one dominating the other, not one controlling the other.

Now, if you think Paul would have had a difficult time trying to bring people together today, just imagine dealing with the Jew and Gentile believers of his time. When the Bible says there was enmity between them, it's talking about war! Why do you think Paul spent so many verses of Scripture saying in so many ways that the blood of Jesus Christ abolished the enmity?

After centuries of being God's chosen people, of being the only nation with whom God would communicate, of course the Jews would want to lead the way when their long-awaited Messiah appeared. They were the only ones who knew about Him. They had been steeped in religious traditions and ceremonies while the Gentiles were worshipping the sun and birds or the Greek or Roman gods. And the Gentile idea of worship was the Jewish idea of depravity! So of course the Jews would believe that they should be the leaders and dominate the Gentile believers. But Paul contended:

> **E**ven when we were dead in sins, hath quickened us together with Christ, (by grace ye are saved;)
> And hath raised us up together, and made us sit together in heavenly places in Christ Jesus.

EPHESIANS 2:5-6

God didn't quicken and raise the body in parts! He raised the whole body up *together.* There are some blessings that you and I will never get until we see everybody with whom we are associated come into that same level of blessing. I'm talking about corporate blessings! We must see the Church as one unit, one body. We must begin to understand that the greater blessing is not on us as individuals, but on the whole corporation for whom Jesus died.

If you ever understand that, it will make an evangelist out of you! You will become obligated and committed to my deliverance because you will realize that you will not be totally whole without me. Why? God has raised us up together! We are intimately and sensitively connected forever in the spirit. I am a living stone connected to you, another living stone, and God will work on us until we fit together!

There is a wonderful illustration of this in Numbers, chapter 32, just before the children of Israel were going to cross the Jordan River and take the promised land. Two of the tribes of Israel wanted to settle where they were and did not want to cross the Jordan and fight with the rest of their brothers and sisters. This was Moses' response:

> **A**nd Moses said unto the children of Gad and to the children of Reuben, Shall your brethren go to war, and shall ye sit here?
> And wherefore discourage ye the heart of the children of Israel from going over into the land which the Lord hath given them?
>
> NUMBERS 32:6-7

When Moses confronted the tribes of Gad and Reuben with their sin, they immediately turned around and came back into the position of unity. They said:

> *We will not return unto our houses, until the children of Israel have inherited every man his inheritance.*
>
> NUMBERS 32:18

The tribes of Gad and Reuben were saying, "We've got to leave our inheritance, cross over to the other side, and fight with our brothers. We will not rest and cannot enjoy what we have until they have theirs. If we are one, all of us have to walk in the faith and the unity of the Spirit to embrace and obtain the inheritance God has given us all."

I can't enjoy my healing while you're sick. I can't enjoy my victory while you're a victim. There's something about me receiving a blessing that makes me have to minister to you and say, "The same God who brought me through can bring you through!" He quickens us and raises us up *together.* We are His workmanship — corporately.

A HABITATION OF GOD

> *In whom ye also are builded together for an habitation of God through the Spirit.*
>
> EPHESIANS 2:22

Please notice this: We are *"builded together* for an habitation of God." Paul is not talking about each

141

of us as individuals in this context. He is speaking of corporate realities. There is a place in God that the Church will never know until we lay aside our petty differences and allow the Holy Spirit to make us one. But there is no way the body of Christ can come together and be one without allowing the Holy Spirit to move on us as a corporate body. Do you see that?

If the Church could be united over doctrine, we have enough learned and respected theologians and seminaries to have accomplished that by now. If we were going to be united by a Christian celebrity, don't you think powerful and dynamic ministers like Billy Graham or John Wesley or Dwight Moody would have achieved unity by now? No, the Word of God tells us that no celebrity will unite us, nor will the great programs and ideas of man. Only the Holy Spirit can unite us, and Paul clearly understood that.

Jesus also understood that, which is why He told the disciples not to go anywhere or to do anything after His ascension until they received the Holy Spirit. (See Luke 24:49.) This is why He spent His last hours before His crucifixion telling the disciples all about the Holy Spirit, the one who would come and be to them exactly what He had been to them. And before He went to the cross, Jesus prayed a long, beautiful prayer for the Church, which would be formed after His resurrection. The theme of that prayer was unity:

> **N**either pray I for these alone, but for them also which shall believe on me through their word;
> That they all may be one; as thou, Father, art in me, and I in thee, that they also may be one in us: that the world may believe that thou hast sent me.
>
> JOHN 17:20-21

The cry of Jesus' heart for His Church is the same today as it was when He prayed this prayer: that we might be one as He and the Father are one. But this concept of unity and oneness — this kind of togetherness — is unfathomable to the natural mind! We can read that verse a million times and nod and say, "Yes, amen, we must be one." But then we look at all the denominations who are at war over this doctrine and that doctrine. We look at all the saints we cannot stand to be around because they're just not living holy enough for us or they are flaky and do stupid things. Then we look at all the preachers who have fallen and given the whole Church a bad reputation. How can we ever be one with all these crazy, mixed-up people!

That's what Ephesians, chapter 2, is all about! Paul says, "Lest you become too good to be fitly framed together with your brethren, just remember how you were once dead in your trespasses and sins. Bring to mind how you walked according to the course of this world and Satan was your spiritual master. Then consider how the Jew and Gentile were at war and how the blood of Jesus abolished that war. And once you see again how only the gracious workmanship of God brought you to salvation and is continuing to save you and make you holy, consider the reality that you were raised and seated with your brothers and sisters — all of them! Now, I know you cannot accomplish this unity in your own strength and ability, and that's why you have the Holy Spirit. That's His job — so let Him do it! When you do, you will see a move of God's power that will shake the world."

It is only the supernatural workmanship of God by His Spirit that will bring us into true unity and oneness. And we are seeing this happen all over the world today. Believers and their leaders are praying and seeking out relationships with believers and leaders from all denominations, all races, and all nationalities. God is moving as never before to bring the body of Christ together because there is a power in corporate worship, in being of one mind, one heart, and one spirit, which will blast through the gates of hell as no nuclear weapon ever demolished a natural site!

Within the hearts of believers across the globe lies more potential power than the world has ever seen, and it is called the love of God in the unity of the Spirit. When we as individual believers simply begin to allow the Holy Spirit free reign in our lives, giving Him permission to clean us up, blow away the cobwebs of our past, and bring forth His righteousness, peace, and joy in our lives, we will love one another! We will be fitly framed together! And Jesus told us that it is this love for one another that will alert the world that God sent Him to be their Lord and Savior.

We will be one with the Father as Jesus is one with the Father. We will be one with each other as we are one with Jesus. Then there is no limit to the surge of God's power that will flow through us to touch those who are lost, broken, hurting, and without hope. This is God's masterful and magnificent workmanship in the Church today. Hallelujah!

REFERENCES

Adam Clarke Commentary. 6 vols. Adam Clarke. *PC Study Bible.* Version 2.1J. CD-ROM. Seattle: Biblesoft, 1993-1998.

Barnes' Notes on the OT & NT. 14 vols. Albert Barnes. *PC Study Bible.* Version 2.1J. CD-ROM. Seattle: Biblesoft, 1993-1998.

The Bible Knowledge Commentary: An Exposition of the Scriptures. Dallas Seminary faculty. Editors, John F. Walvoord, Roy B. Zuck. Wheaton, IL: Victor Books. 1983-1985. Published in electronic form by Logos Research Systems Inc., 1996.

Brown, Driver, & Briggs' Definitions. Francis Brown, D.D., D. Litt., S. R. Driver, D.D., D. Litt., and Charles A. Briggs, D.D., D. Litt. *PC Study Bible.* Version 2.1J. CD-ROM. Seattle: Biblesoft, 1993-1998.

Expositor's Bible Commentary, New Testament. Frank E. Gaebelein, General Editor. J. D. Douglas, Associate Editor. Grand Rapids, MI: Zondervan Publishing House, 1976-1992.

A Greek-English Lexicon of the New Testament and Other Early Christian Literature. Walter Bauer. Second edition, revised and augmented by F. W. Gingrich, Fredrick Danker from Walter Bauer's fifth edition. Chicago and London: The University of Chicago Press, 1958.

The Greek New Testament. Editor Kurt Aland, et al. CD-ROM of the 3rd edition, corrected. Federal Republic of Germany: United Bible Societies, 1983. Published in electronic form by Logos Research Systems, Inc. 1996.

Greek (UBS) text and Hebrew (BHS) text. PC Study Bible. Version 2.1J. CD-ROM. Seattle: Biblesoft, 1993-1998.

The Hebrew-Greek Key Study Bible. Compiled and edited by Spiros Zodhiates, Th.D. World Bible Publishers, Inc., 1984, 1991.

Interlinear Bible. *PC Study Bible.* Version 2.1J. CD-ROM Seattle: Biblesoft, 1993-1998.

Jamieson, Fausset & Brown Commentary. 6 vols. Robert Jamieson, A. R. Fausset, and David Brown. *PC Study Bible.* Version 2.1J. CD-ROM. Seattle: Biblesoft, 1993-1998.

A Manual Grammar of the Greek New Testament. H. E. Dana, Th.D. and Julius R. Mantey. Toronto, Canada: MacMillan Publishing Company, 1927.

Matthew Henry's Commentary. 6 vols. Matthew Henry. *PC Study Bible.* Version 2.1J. CD-ROM. Seattle: Biblesoft, 1993-1998.

The New Linguistic and Exegetical Key to the Greek New Testament. Fritz Reineker, Revised version by Cleon Rogers and Cleon Rogers III. Grand Rapids, MI: Zondervan Publishing Company, 1998.

Strong's Exhaustive Concordance of the Bible. J. B. Strong. *PC Study Bible.* Version 2.1J. CD-ROM. Seattle: Biblesoft, 1993-1998.

Vincent's Word Studies in the NT. 4 vols. Marvin R. Vincent, D.D. *PC Study Bible.* Version 2.1J. CD-ROM. Seattle: Biblesoft, 1993-1998.

Wuest's Word Studies from the Greek New Testament for the English Reader. Volume One, Ephesians. Kenneth S. Wuest. Grand Rapids, MI: Wm. B. Eerdmans Publishing Company, 1953.

ABOUT THE AUTHOR

T. D. Jakes is the founder and senior pastor of The Potter's House church in Dallas, Texas. A highly celebrated author with several bestselling books to his credit, he frequently ministers in massive crusades and conferences across the nation. His weekly television broadcast is viewed nationally in millions of homes. Bishop Jakes lives in Dallas with his wife, Serita, and their five children.

To contact T. D. Jakes, write:
T. D. Jakes Ministries
International Communications Center
P. O. Box 210887
Dallas, Texas 75211

or visit his Web site at:
www.tdjakes.org

Books by T.D. Jakes

Six Pillars From Ephesians

Loved by God • Experiencing Jesus
Intimacy With God • Life Overflowing
Celebrating Marriage • Overcoming the Enemy

Lay Aside the Weight
Lay Aside the Weight Workbook & Journal
Loose That Man & Let Him Go!
Devotions from Loose That Man & Let Him Go!
Loose That Man & Let Him Go! With Workbook
So You Call Yourself a Man?
T. D. Jakes Speaks to Men!
T. D. Jakes Speaks to Women!
Woman, Thou Art Loosed!
Woman, Thou Art Loosed! Devotional

Videos by T.D. Jakes

The Insights on Ephesians Series (Six Videos)
Rock for the Thirsty Soul
Praise in the Midst of Pain
Overcoming Your Limitations
Talk Your Way Out

REFLECT THE
Radiance
OF THE MASTER

The Princess Within by Serita Ann Jakes

The Princess Within is an honest, intimate book
from Serita Jakes that helps women reflect the glory of
God as they live every day. Filled with her own stories
of struggles and triumphs, it offers tender wisdom
for every woman.

Whether you are burdened by past failures or simply
trying to draw as near to God as possible, this book will
give you the insight and strength you need.

BETHANYHOUSE

YOU SEE ORDINARY GOD SEES

Extraordinary!

Expounding on five encouraging life stories of men in the Bible, T. D. Jakes helps you realize that God created you to be free, powerful, and filled with purpose. You *can experience* deep intimacy with Him. You can become a powerful instrument of His love and reconciliation, both to the church and to a dying world.

So You Call Yourself a Man? will strengthen your faith in God's love and purpose for you. Remember, you may see yourself as ordinary, but God sees your extraordinary potential. Unlock it today!

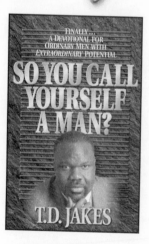

So You Call Yourself a Man?
by T. D. Jakes